CHALLENGES

Challenges

A Memoir of My Life in Opera

SARAH CALDWELL

With Rebecca Matlock

Wesleyan University Press
Middletown, Connecticut

Published by Wesleyan University Press, Middletown, CT 06459

www.wesleyan.edu/wespress

© 2008 by Rebecca Matlock

Printed in the United States of America

5 4 3 2 1

All photographs by Rebecca Matlock.

Frontispiece: The Opera House on Washington Street

Library of Congress Cataloging-in-Publication Data

Caldwell, Sarah, 1924–2006.

Challenges : a memoir of my life in opera / Sarah Caldwell with
Rebecca Matlock.

p.   cm.

Includes index.

ISBN 978-0-8195-6885-4 (cloth : alk. paper)

1. Caldwell, Sarah, 1924–2006.

2. Conductors (Music)—United States—Biography.

3. Opera producers and directors—United States—Biography.

I. Matlock, Rebecca.

II. Title.

ML422.C225A3 2008

782.1092—dc22   2008007653

[B]

To Members of the Opera Company of Boston

Contents

Foreword

Rebecca Matlock

To approach Sarah Caldwell's home in Lincoln, Massachusetts, you turned right past a nondescript mailbox and traveled along a narrow road through a meadow until you reached a circular driveway. There you were confronted by an extraordinary poured-concrete house with many angles and huge surfaces of glass.

The interior of the house was full of surprises. The first thing you saw as you entered the contemporary house was an antique table. It was ponderous and elegant. It had been used in the law

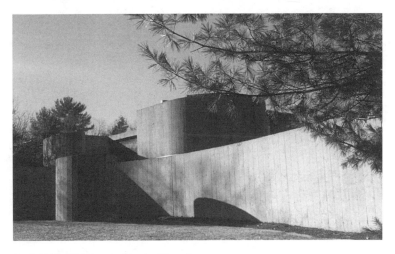

Sarah Caldwell's House in Lincoln, Massachusetts

office of Sarah's great-uncle, Ed, who was responsible for some of her best childhood memories.

Behind it on a lower level was the living room. In it sat a delicate rocking chair that had been passed down through several generations of her family. Sarah said that she hoped no one would sit in it and no one did.

Nearby was a Steinway grand piano. It had been bought for Sarah's mother by her parents as a present when she graduated with a music degree from Northwestern University. It enabled Margaret to perform as a concert pianist and to give music lessons in order to help support the family after her father's bank failed during the Depression. Soon after the bank's failure, her father died.

Sarah loved the house and bought it at the suggestion of her financial adviser even though it was expensive and much too large for someone who never married. It was a perfect house, though, to

Sarah relaxes at home

Sarah entertains at home

Sarah's white dog, "Cranberry," in the backyard

share with her mother, who was by then confined to a wheelchair. Ramps connected the various levels. There was only one staircase and it was made of cast concrete.

The interior walls and ceilings of that unique house were also made of concrete, as were the floors. The concrete floors were heated so Sarah could enjoy padding around barefoot all year round. Because there were no straight lines in the house, Sarah contracted with a person who designed interiors for yachts to make contoured bookshelves for her collection of books on many subjects in many languages. There were no windows, as the exterior walls themselves were windows.

There were no doors except pocket doors for the bathrooms. All the various spaces—Sarah's office, the kitchen and dining rooms, her music studio, the bedrooms, and the small room with a fireplace—all flowed from one to the other. There were no closed shelves.

Light poured into unexpected places that contained plants and stones. Those light wells were designed for the house by Buckminster Fuller, the architect who invented the geodesic dome. The house had

Jim Morgan enjoys her extensive library

Sarah confers with John Cunningham, her business manager

Herbert Senn, a creative set designer for the Opera Company of Boston

Helen Pond collaborated with Herbert Senn to design memorable sets

been built in 1965 by architects Thomas and Mary McNatz for their family. Sarah bought it in 1979.

The first piece of furniture Sarah acquired when she could afford her own place to live was a Scandinavian chair. She bought it even before she invested in a bed and slept in it for a night. Through the years she continued to buy classic Scandinavian furniture for her house.

Decorations were related to her opera productions. There were exquisite three-dimensional light boxes representing sets from different operas she produced. There was a wall hanging by the Israeli set designer David Sharir, who had devised sets for some of her most popular productions. She also exhibited a ryijy wall hanging that she had commissioned me to make to commemorate Making Music Together, a musical exchange between American musicians, composers, and performers and those of the Soviet Union.

Sometimes Sarah auditioned new compositions at home. The house was adapted to be acoustically friendly, including the addition of strips of wood to the ceilings by her friend Bob Newman, who taught acoustics at the Massachusetts Institute of Technology.

Sometimes symphonic music would flow through the connected spaces, but just as often there would be the muffled sounds of a tennis match, or of earnest voices on Court TV, which she loved to watch. Sarah could sit anywhere in the house and make requests or give instructions to her staff and be heard perfectly everywhere.

When her friends were entertained at dinner (a repast seldom cooked by the hostess herself), wonderful food was served, enhanced by carefully selected wines.

When I came to Lincoln to help record reminiscences for this book, I stayed in a bedroom with a glass wall overlooking a pond that had its own pair of loons. I heard them but I never saw them. Descendants of Edgar Allan Poe's ravens strutted about. Sarah's white fuzzy dog, Cranberry, liked to chase them.

My room never appeared the same. Each time it felt like a stage set for a different opera. Table settings, particularly those for breakfast, often had the charm of miniature stage sets. They incorporated, besides flowers, gifts and purchases from Sarah's travels.

I suspect this attention to detail was in part because her colleague Jim Morgan, who shared the house with her, took special care to keep Sarah happy and productive and to make her guest feel welcome.

I consider Sarah's house a metaphor not only for her incomparable presentations, but for Sarah herself. It was erudite, full of mystery and excitement, unexpectedness, creativity and warmth.

CHALLENGES

IN BOSTON

Sarah approached recording her memoir as if she were staging an opera. How it would develop would become clear as it progressed. Just as it was important to have a concept for each of her productions, it was important to have a concept for her book. She chose to share and emphasize what was unique in her experience.

The creation of a narrative of threads that would be woven together to become a long, logical line would produce chapters that grew out of ideas with comments supporting those ideas. She didn't want simply to string anecdotes together.

Leitmotifs would appear and reappear in the narrative as musical phrases do in music. One of these was the importance of research for understanding what the composer wanted to project, in order to increase the depth of understanding of the performers, and ultimately, of the audience. To emphasize this concern, the Music Theater Research Foundation was included in her will.

Another basic concern was fund-raising. Fund-raising could be made interesting, she insisted. It was important to emphasize that it is vital to the stability and even to the survival of opera. There was not a day, she confessed, when she was not filled with terror that there would not be enough money for what she wanted to do. Sarah envied musical organizations that were supported and subsidized by their governments, and she thought ours should be as well.

At first Mrs. Tom Cabot of Boston was referred to simply as "a sweet lady who thought Boston should have an opera company, the woman who helped the Opera Company of Boston get its start financially." Later, it was decided that she should be mentioned by name: it was thanks to her—and to her friends who matched her contributions—that it became possible for the Opera Group to begin performing. Mrs. Cabot hosted a series of teas to which she invited her friends, who always contributed a few hundred dollars; once, when she included a newcomer to Boston, that person gave $10,000.

Key performers in the orchestra were sometimes selected and rehearsed by Sarah herself, who never forgot that it was the orchestra that was performing, not the conductor.

It was important that costumes be appropriate and sets be challenging and constructive. Working closely with costume and set designers, she was constantly challenged to determine the most creative and to persuade them to work on her terms. Without dictating what they should do, but paying attention to every detail, Sarah, as artistic director, didn't hesitate to make suggestions before approving their designs.

Operatic performers were auditioned in venues that approximated the acoustical surroundings vocalists would experience in live performances. Most often these auditions took place in New York, though sometimes in Boston. The voices of the singers had to be excellent. The performers had to be in good physical condition, be the correct age, and look right for their parts. They had to be able to act as well as to sing.

Communication was the most important concept of all. Over and over again Sarah's comments illustrate how musicians, regardless of their political and social affiliation, communicate with each other and with their audiences through music.

Sarah Caldwell's memoir was written for friends and for aficionados of symphonic music and opera. She does not talk down to her readers. Details of plots of operas, except for those not well known, are seldom mentioned. Sometimes it was difficult to get her to discuss even those. Her opinion was that if the readers didn't know the plot, they could look it up. Once when I suggested that she might want to explain Bayreuth, she asked, "Why?"

Instead of presenting her thoughts chronologically, she preferred free association. Productions that were separated by several years were sometimes compared. She was casual about dates, assuming once again that, if someone really wanted to know, that person could check the chronology of her performances.

Several of the premiere performances were not mentioned at all because Sarah wanted to hold something back for her next book. The earliest, a world premiere, in 1961, was *Command Performance* by Robert Middleton. Between 1975 and 1986 American premieres included, in addition to those discussed, *Benvenuto Cellini*, by Hector Berlioz, *Stiffelio*, by Giuseppe Verdi, *Ice Break* by Sir Michael Tippett, *Die Soldaten* by Bernd Alois Zimmerman, and *Taverner*, by Peter Maxwell Davies. First names of composers are seldom mentioned in the memoir.

The narrative begins not with the first opera Sarah Caldwell conducted, which was Bedřich Smetana's *The Bartered Bride*, but with *Voyage to the Moon*, an opera by Jacques Offenbach which was based on the Jules Verne novel *De la terre à la lune*. Translated freely from French (even the title was changed a bit) and adapted by Sarah and her friend from Arkansas, Eugene Haun, it was a smash hit from its first performance. At the beginning of the American space program, the timing could not have been better. She was invited to tour it across the country and present it not once, but twice, at the White House.

Chapter 1

The Boston Public Garden

＋‖‥＊‥＊‥‖＋

When the imagination of Americans had been ignited by the possibility of travel in space—including the preposterous idea that
someday someone might actually visit the Moon—our fledgling
Opera Group presented Jacques Offenbach's comic opera, *The
Voyage to the Moon.* Startlingly appropriate for the time, it was the hit
of the 1958 Boston Arts Festival. *Time* magazine praised the first-
rate cast, and the *Boston Daily Globe* exclaimed that "the roar you
may have heard was not from a space ship; it was a standing ovation from the large festival crowd!" The *Boston Herald* predicted
that the Public Garden would not be big enough to hold all the
Bostonians who would hear about the performance and want to
see it.

The Public Garden was the ideal place from which to launch
that first production. Together with the adjacent Boston Common, it forms a large park in the center of Boston with small gardens full of carefully tended flowers. Paths lead to various parts of
the gardens where stand a number of statues of distinguished and
less distinguished citizens of the past. There are pools large
enough for swan boats to float in the spring and summer.

In the springtime, in the open space in the center of the Public
Garden, the festival held there included visual arts displayed in a
series of tents set up especially for the purpose. On a partially covered wooden stage (reconstructed each year), opera, ballet, symphony concerts and dance concerts, some by international performers, including Moscow's Moiseyev Dancers, were performed.

More than a thousand people could attend each night, and the festival continued for several weeks.

Because the festival was financed by city funds with contributions from merchants and philanthropists who were supportive of the arts, the sale of tickets was forbidden. The only way the public could help the festival financially was by renting chairs. While most people sat in rented chairs, those who preferred to do so brought blankets and relaxed on the grass. If the weather was good, everything was lovely, but as the festival took place in late May and early June (months often marked by rainy spells), every performance had a rain date.

Encouraged by the possibility that America could put a man on the moon during the next decade, the exploration of space was very much at the heart of our consciousness. This was particularly true in Boston, where much of the scientific work that would make space exploration possible was being carried out.

When the Opera Group was invited to participate in the arts festival, I saw it as a perfect opportunity to present *Voyage to the Moon*. I had wanted to stage that amusing light opera, which Jacques Offenbach based on Jules Verne's science fiction classic about Earth people visiting the Moon, since discovering material in the Boston Public Library about the original 1875 Paris production. I had found detailed information, including sketches for sets and costumes, in handsome leather-bound books housed so high on the shelves that a ladder was necessary to bring them down.

We were informed that our participation, which would include a radio broadcast of the opening performance, would be funded primarily by the Boston Arts Festival—but it was expected that we also contribute to the cost. With sublime confidence we decided that all we needed to be successful was promotion and publicity.

The Opera Group voted to use $5,000 that had been given to us by Mrs. Cabot, the lady who became our first major benefactress. In addition, during a hot summer, wearing my navy suit with a white blouse that I laundered every night, by making up to six calls a day I had managed to elicit an extra $100 for start-up money for a serious fund-raising campaign.

Jeopardizing our painfully accumulated nest egg by paying $12,000 toward costumes to be custom-made in Boston and in New York was a nerve-wracking experience. Although they cost a tiny fraction of what they would cost today, I never felt so sinful in my life. The costumes were based on meticulous sketches I had found in the Boston Library. Among the visual material were detailed drawings of the Jules Verne cannon out of which the space ship was shot in which the Earth people traveled to the moon.

Because of the attention-getting work he was doing at the Brattle Theatre in Boston, we selected Robert Fletcher to be both costume and set designer. He did not disappoint us. The Moon people became odd-looking individuals who wore witty and creative clothing including colorful leotards, aprons, cassocks, and even bustles while Earth people wore more conventional clothing.

We auditioned singers in New York and in Boston and quickly assembled the cast. Many of the people who participated I had known at Tanglewood, where the Boston Symphony Orchestra performed during the summer, and others had sung with the New England Opera Theater with which I had also been associated.

My great friend Bob Joffrey, full of sparkling ideas and enthusiasm, came to Boston to choreograph the production. Dancers from his Robert Joffrey Theatre Ballet were among the inhabitants of Earth and Moon in our production. As there was weak gravity on the moon, everybody moved about in a sort of floating manner.

Poet Eugene Haun, a friend since student days in Arkansas, and I manipulated the text of the libretto (which I had translated into English) of the romantic comedy about people from Earth visiting the Moon. We tightened the plot to suit our purposes. We worked on the dialogue, revising and editing until the last minute. The result was a free adaptation from the original. The music is charming and ebullient and amusing; it is spirited and touching, but not sacred. I did not feel uncomfortable changing the sequence of events and making cuts because it was incredibly long.

We cast handsome baritone Donald Gramm as King of the Earth, and bass Jim Billings, a brilliant comedian, as King of the Moon. They were wonderful together. Two outstanding young singing actors, David Lloyd and Adelaide Bishop, sang the romantic leads. Norman Kelly sang the part of Dr. Blastoff, the scientist with rockets in his head, with bravado.

Robert Fletcher used the "pereactos" design for the construction of the set. That's a Greek scenic discipline in which you have a triangle with several pieces that fit on to it. Each time the triangle moves the audience sees a different aspect of it. Included in our production were four triangles in front of a rectangular backstage. Each triangle was a separate room and the singers could step from one to the other. The sets were constructed with sliding panels that could be changed instantly with the assistance of eight muscular stagehands pushing simultaneously in the same direction.

On my conductor's stand was a little light. At a certain place in the score I would punch a button that turned on the warning light, alerting the stagehands to go to their positions. When I punched a second button the warning light was turned off, signaling that they were to put their hands on the place where they were going to push. The instant the warning light came back on, they pushed. This was probably the first time that the stage manager's position was in the pit, at the railing.

Timeliness was the secret of our success. The quality of the period flavor of the piece was what made it wonderful. It was the combination of this and the silliness of it and yet our real-life determination to go to the Moon and the moon shot that we were feverishly preparing for in the United States that made it timely. The *Jewish Advocate* called ours "a launching calculated to make the efforts of the boys at Cape Canaveral look feeble."

We became an instant success. *Voyage to the Moon* was reviewed in *Time* magazine and the *New York Times*. Columbia Artists Management, then considered the gods of the music industry, offered to book a national tour and we accepted their offer. Between January and April 1959, we performed in many cities in more than half the states.

It was a bus-and-truck tour. About sixty people traveled in a lumbering bus and two trucks and a van. The stagehands slept either in the van or in the truck. We did six shows, sometimes seven shows, a week. The union controlled very carefully how much we could do. We could ride only two hundred miles, maybe two hundred and fifty miles, each day. We'd get up at eight o'clock in the morning and get on the bus. We'd get out and we'd be in the place where we were going to perform that night.

Our stagehands would have left the night before and slept, set the scenery up by noon, and gone to sleep again. That way by evening we could be ready to give a show. It was very exciting for a while but after we had been on the bus by day and stayed in inexpensive motels night after night for several weeks, it got to be depressing. People became kind of cross but nobody dropped out.

Midway during the tour I got a telephone call from the treasurer of the Opera Group, informing me that he and the president wanted me to come back at once. I shouldn't have left the tour because I was the conductor, but we did have an assistant conductor; it was such an urgent call I felt I had to return to Boston.

I was confronted by the entire board. Everybody looked ominous. I couldn't think for the life of me what the matter could be. The treasurer pulled out a telephone bill and said, "What do you know about this?" It was a telephone bill for an enormous amount of money, thousands of dollars. Most of it was for long-distance calls to Las Vegas from our phone. It was so preposterous I just laughed. They were not amused.

He said, "We aren't accusing you personally of having made these calls but you have been duped. There are people in the company who are running up gambling bills and doing things."

And I said, "It's not possible! That's ridiculous. It is not possible that we could have had such a telephone bill. Has anybody asked the telephone company about it? This has to be a mistake. This has to be someone else's bill. Something is wrong!"

I insisted on calling the telephone company then and there. Well, as it turned out, our office was across the street from a little hotel and somehow the wires had gotten crossed and we had the hotel's bill for the month.

I thought because we were bringing this wonderful company from Boston the people there would be very proud. We got marvelous reviews. We cut them out. We sent them back to our trustees and basic supporters. I soon learned, though, that all the nice letters I had been writing back and the reviews we had been sending from all over America were not what my board wanted. What they wanted was opera in Boston. It soon became obvious that unless we performed at home, interest there would quickly dissipate.

During that tour across America I came to realize that every opera, for me, would be a voyage somewhere, and that while I was searching for one specific thing I would be likely to find something else. What I determined to do with each production was to share the journey. On the stage my ambition would be to present the place, the time, the ideas, the problems, and the solutions that the composer and the librettist revealed when they wrote the opera.

Through opera I determined to try to create a sense of kinship with our artistic ancestors. I operate on the theory that they were not fools. Although an opera, especially a comic opera such as *Voyage to the Moon,* may seem silly, if it was written by an intelligent person or intelligent collaborators, then it is not silly. One has to give credit for sensible attitudes of our musical predecessors and not laugh at them. This is particularly true, I believe, when period instruments and period ornamentation are used.

An example of this is an opera by Handel that was first performed in London early in the eighteenth century called *Orlando*. The opera becomes more interesting when we learn that as an entrepreneur Handel frequently wrote music incorporating the use of unusual stage machinery. Curiosity about the effects that resulted from this practice brought more and more people to his theater. He bought a cloud machine and an exploding volcano, both of which were used in *Orlando*.

Our tour with *Voyage to the Moon* was instructive and fun, challenging and enervating, but in the end disappointing, because we did not receive the infusion of cash that we expected. One might say that although our opera company got a jump start to the Moon that provided us with exhilaration, it didn't sustain life. In fact, during our thirteen-week tour the production lost money and we almost lost our shirts. From then on we realized that we had to take fund-raising very, very seriously.

We were yet to learn that even if we had not reached the financial goal we had set for ourselves, we should begin to perform; otherwise the interest that we had carefully generated would be dissipated. Moments of desperation because of the specter of not being able to raise enough money for our activities would remain central to our creative lives, never ceasing to haunt us.

Several years later, in March 1967, we were invited by President Lyndon Johnson to present a shortened version of *Voyage to the Moon* to honor President Cevdet Sunay of Turkey and his wife during their official visit to Washington. In their honor we had some of the songs translated and sung in Turkish.

Resplendent in red and blue uniforms, the United States Marine Corps Band sat in the hallway outside the East Room. Conducting in sedate black, I kept one eye on them and the other on what was going on on the stage. Afterward the band leader whispered to me that we had won the sweepstakes by keeping the president awake longer than any other cultural presentation.

That evening I became the first woman to conduct at the White House as well as the first woman to conduct the United States Marine Corps Band.

Voyage to the Moon obviously made a big impression on the Johnsons because just before the launching of the manned Apollo 8 flight in December 1968, we were invited to return to the White House to present it a second time.

The performers came to Boston for special rehearsals and we were invited to come to Washington a day early so we could rehearse at the White House. For our production we had help from some of the astronauts themselves. We discussed with them what they would be taking on their mission to encircle the moon, what they would have for breakfast before they boarded, what they would eat during their voyage to the Moon, things like that. Our performers had the same, so that caused a lot of amusement.

At the White House rehearsal I explained that we would like to use psychedelic projections on the ceiling for moon ambience. I suspect my use of the word "psychedelic" was the reason why my request was refused, but the security people said it was because the Kodak projector that would have been set up behind the president's back could contain a weapon.

One of the stagehands asked a member of the White House staff if there was a coffee vending machine somewhere. Almost immediately an elaborate silver service arrived, with coffee for everyone. Sipping our coffee from elegant White House cups, set designer Helen Pond and I decided that our buying white gloves to wear to the White House had been justified.

Before our performance one of the cast members told me that he planned when President and Mrs. Johnson came to the stage after the performance to thank us, to present them with a recording he had made of "Pray for Peace" and that he hoped that his picture would be taken doing this. This was during the Vietnam

War, when there was a great deal of criticism of our involvement there. He was quite a sincere young man who probably had no idea of the enormity of what he was planning to do. I told him he simply must not do it. He said, "Oh, it'll be all right. Don't worry!"

I was really concerned, so I told Donald Gramm, the lead member of the cast, what the situation was. Donald had the wit to understand that this could have become a really awkward incident, so he said, "Don't worry. Let me take care of it. Don't say anything. Don't do anything. Just give me a few minutes." He went down to the dressing room and soon came back saying, "It's all taken care of. It won't happen."

I asked, "Donald, what did you do?" and he said, "I bought it!"

The guest of honor was James Webb, head of the National Aeronautics and Space Administration, who that night received the Presidential Medal of Freedom, our nation's highest civilian award. Among the guests were the famous woman pilot of World War II, Jacqueline Cochran, and rocket scientist Wernher von Braun.

Lady Bird Johnson, introducing our presentation, suggested that we all fasten our seat belts for Boston's version of a voyage to the moon. In this special performance Moon people wore black-and-white plastic clothing while Fantasia, the Princess of the Moon, a black Washington opera singer whose name was Lauretta Young, wore a silver miniskirt with silver stockings. Earth people wore frock coats.

As they are ready to blast off in the rocket, a big cylinder with double doors, a fuse is lit. It starts to run. The curtain comes down. The fuse continues to run across the blackout curtain. High up on the proscenium appears Earth on one side and on the other side the Moon. A tiny spaceship starts going from Earth toward the Moon. There's a cloud in the center. The spaceship goes behind the cloud and that's intermission. That curtain later became part of the memorabilia at the Lyndon Johnson Presidential Library in Austin.

After intermission, we are on the Moon, where the inhabitants are talking and reacting. They have telescopes and they see something coming. The little spaceship goes until it hits the Moon with an explosion. The Moon people run away and the Earth people come out of their spacecraft.

They soon get acquainted. A conversation between the Earth King and the Moon King that the audience giggled about afterward was when the leaders discussed such things as money. The King of the Earth asks the King of the Moon, "What do you use for money?" The King of the Moon asks, "What's money?" and the King of the Earth answers, "That's what the liberals say!" Then the King of the Moon asks, "What are liberals?" The King of the Earth explains, "We have liberals and we have conservatives; the liberals are to the left of the road and the conservatives are to the right." The punchline comes when the King of the Moon asks, "Where are we going?"

Chapter 2

The Little Opera House

That question, "Where are we going?" was one that applied both practically and aesthetically to the Opera Group. After our initial success in the Boston Public Garden during the Arts Festival of 1958, we required a place where we could rehearse and perform. We also needed an audience to attend our performances. We decided that the Fine Arts Theater, which we rechristened the Little Opera House, would be the most appropriate place available to us for our performances.

The Little Opera House was a small theater on a side street. It was part of a larger building known as the Back Bay or Donnelly Theater located on Massachusetts Avenue up a couple of blocks from Symphony Hall. To enter the theater it was necessary to walk up a flight of stairs. We spruced it up. We cleaned and painted and laid carpets.

The opening date for Giacomo Puccini's always popular *La bohème* was January 29, 1959, almost exactly two years after a small group of people got together in my apartment to discuss the feasibility of establishing a new opera company in Boston.

From the beginning we set for ourselves the goal of creating an opera company that would present operatic productions of the highest level. We wanted our productions to have meaning for today, for tomorrow, and for yesterday. Our aim was to establish a permanent professional company of first-rank singers, instrumentalists, designers, directors, conductors, managers, composers, and librettists, and to provide them with an artistic climate in which they would have the opportunity to achieve their highest potential. This goal, although we would find it difficult to achieve, we always kept in mind.

Our second goal was to make our organization financially self-sustaining. This became a tremendously pressure-laden ongoing exercise. I never experienced a day without terror that we would not be able to meet our financial obligations.

We were honored when composer Igor Stravinsky agreed to be our honorary chairman.

We decided that the best way to raise funds would be to dramatize our plans as well as our need for money and to involve as many people as we could. In order to get things moving we began a citywide drive for grassroots support. We started with a kickoff dinner at the Copley Plaza Hotel in Boston for six hundred people, including the governor.

Using volunteer workers we launched a week of what we called Operation Opera. Modeled on a Community Concerts program for building audiences, it was a plan for systematically widening personal contacts who, with their friends and acquaintances, would support our membership drive. With indispensable help from radio, TV, and the press, during ten days we recruited thousands of members each of whom paid ten dollars to join and to attend a performance of *La bohème* and two other operas. Only members could attend the performances and there would be no reserved seats. The reason our decision to raise capital from direct contributions worked, I am sure, was that people agreed to give one week, not the rest of their lives, to the endeavor.

Rather than a manager, we had a committee made up of prominent businessmen who met weekly and discussed in great seriousness such things as whether lemonade or champagne or both should be offered for sale and, if so, how much we should charge and how it was to be sold. A house manager named Walter was engaged and Walter's duties were much discussed and analyzed; he was instructed to provide careful written reports on every move he made. We learned a lot about the importance of attention to detail in doing business during meetings with that group.

We put together, I think, a really beautiful production. It was carefully integrated. We had an excellent orchestra. The musicians were members of the Boston Symphony whom I personally selected. Singers in the chorus were from Boston; many of them had been my students at Boston University. We worked carefully to maintain the balance between the voices and the sound of the orchestra.

I auditioned the principal singers in New York. The artists whom we engaged came to Boston and stayed several weeks. Next door to our theater was a hotel, the Gardner Hotel. This was where most of them stayed. I moved in as well.

Our Mimì was a lovely, dark-haired Canadian soprano named Lois Marshall who had a gorgeous voice with the brilliance that the role demands. Lois had been afflicted by polio and was terribly nervous about being on the stage. All the cast were wonderful to Lois. The procedure was that she would come across the street to the theater and the young men would carry her up the stairs into the theater.

The men in the cast included Donald Gramm, who had been so important to the success of *The Voyage to the Moon;* Robert Trehy, an American singer who came back from Germany and Austria especially to sing with us; Robert Mesrobian; and Hawaiian tenor Charles K. L. Davis, who sang and acted the romantic lead, Rodolfo, with assurance and passion.

David Hayes created an extraordinary set. The stage was redesigned so that it came out into the audience to form a kind of V. The orchestra sat on either side of the V with the conductor more or less at the point, which meant that we had a thrust stage for our first *La bohème.* The stage furnished a real challenge. All movement in that tiny space was carefully planned to take advantage of every inch. The attic room in which the poet, the painter, the philosopher, and the musician lived in cold and poverty was very small. It was necessary for them to go in and out of the room. There had to be a stove where they could light a fire. Each of the young men had a small hunk of the room that included a place to sleep. In their limited areas each placed the stuff he felt he needed and it was up to him to figure out where it could be fitted in.

Colline, the philosopher, used an old mattress with a sheet of plywood on top of his books to support it. Robert Mesrobian, who sang the part of Schaunard, the musician, said he had enjoyed sleeping in a hammock as a child, so he strung a hammock so close to his upright piano that it touched. Costumes for the urchins, hawkers, and crowds of people milling about were as carefully crafted as were those of the leading singers. The frenetic Latin Quarter became the Café Momus when a curtain was drawn.

Although several singers sang the role of Mimi's capricious friend, Musetta, we used basically the same cast for all the performances, which were presented alternately in Italian and in English.

Because the Little Opera House seated only five hundred people, it took sixteen performances of *La bohème* for all the people who were entitled to see it to come to a production. Our $90,000 disappeared very quickly and we were once again scrambling for money.

The opening night audience was so appreciative that even the orchestra received a standing ovation. Curtain calls went on and on. The reviewers were kind (even though one said the loft where the young men lived looked more like a tool shed than a garret). One observed that if the level of our *Bohème* was maintained that the Opera Group would achieve a notable and completely deserved reputation.

The theater critic for the Boston *Daily Record,* described how after a few years of dreaming and working we had created a project for Bostonians to admire and cherish. He praised the sets and remarked that the orchestra, crowded into a pit that reached from wall to wall, played the glorious music of *La bohème* as if they played for the sheer fun of being involved, and that the entire company enjoyed themselves as much as the audience, which went home full of incredulity and enthusiasm.

We did *La bohème* on a tiny budget although it included members of the Boston Symphony and a very fine cast. Nevertheless, I was called before the board and given a dressing-down for spending too much money. Today only one performance of *La bohème* would cost more than all sixteen performances did in 1959.

That first *Bohème* became a metaphor for my personal commitment to opera and to what opera came to mean to Boston. We presented *La bohème* many times over the years and audiences always flocked to see it.

Several years later, in 1966, when we were performing in a real theater, we invited Renata Tebaldi to sing the part of Mimì in *La bohème* in a new production that was designed by the German designer Rudolph Heinrich.

I had met Rudolph Heinrich when he was designing sets for the Komische Oper in East Berlin. After the Berlin Wall went up in 1962, he and his wife, an American singer, made a hectic escape. When I heard that he had left, I tried very hard to get in touch with him and finally did, in Munich, where he had become a professor at the Academy of Music. He ultimately designed sets for Munich, for Covent Garden, and for the Metropolitan Opera.

His concept in designing the set for our *La bohème* was to create a sense of reality. He built a little house on top of a roof. The singers could go outside of it, and they could walk on the rest of the roof. There were chimneys. There were stairs that led down. He used another device that I thought was quite effective. He painted over blowups of photographs of Paris creating a montage that produced a sense of reality that was wondrous.

We discussed Heinrich's approach for staging the production with Renata Tebaldi before she agreed to come to Boston. Nevertheless, two weeks before the opening, while staying at the Ritz-Carlton Hotel overlooking the Public Garden, she became so frightened at the prospect of singing in a set that was different from the one to which she was accustomed that she felt that she couldn't sing a note.

Finally she telephoned to say that she had brought her costumes and wigs and that she would like for us to pick them up. I knew those costumes so I suggested that I bring Rudolph Heinrich to meet her. For Tebaldi he demonstrated his carefully crafted set model, showing her how it was going to work. Our enthusiasm about the production had its effect on her. As she looked at the model, she got excited too. After a time she said, "Obviously, I can't wear my costumes."

Rudolph Heinrich, one of the most perceptive and responsive people with whom I ever worked, said, "May I come tomorrow and bring costume sketches for you?" He was a very, very quick painter and he made two enormous paintings of his costumes that night. The face looked like Tebaldi. He took them to her the next day. She was thrilled, and decided she could come and rehearse.

The first time she came to a rehearsal it was in a chauffeur-driven limousine and she was accompanied by her manager. The set was already constructed on the stage. We worked with her for four or five hours during which she concentrated seriously. Soon she sent the manager away.

She got along well with her Rodolfo, a young Spanish tenor with expressive brown eyes who was making one of his first American appearances. When I auditioned Plácido Domingo in his manager's studio, he played the piano and he sang. It was obvious that he was a wonderful musician. He worked very hard and was terribly nice to Tebaldi. The age difference made it even more intense somehow. Many years later Plácido Domingo said that the staging for act 3 was the most "persuasive" he had ever experienced.

During rehearsals it was our practice for people to go for coffee and snacks. After three or four days Renata Tebaldi went out and got coffee for everybody because she saw that we took turns doing it. After five or six days she helped carry costumes into the theater from the truck to the dressing room. She became comfortable with her colleagues, who treated her like she was one of them, not a great diva.

What I try to do when I direct is create an atmosphere in which people are encouraged to devise things. Tebaldi wasn't used to that but we encouraged her, so she did some unusual things. She was cooperative, she acted the part well, and she sounded fantastic. Mimì died in a chair rather than on the bed. She liked that.

When I worked with distinguished and well-known performers, such as Renata Tebaldi, I discovered that they are interested in working hard and rehearsing and are the most patient of all the cast. They are receptive because that's how they got to be so good. I find generally that it is easier to work with people of this kind than with people who are not so well known but who are on the way up. If they are somewhere in the middle ranks they can behave as if they are terribly grand.

By the time of the Tebaldi-Domingo *La bohème*, the Opera Group had become the Opera Company of Boston, and we were performing in a much larger theater, one that seated 2,500 people. The Back Bay Theater, a former vaudeville house when it was donated to the Boston archdiocese of the Catholic Church by a wealthy family named Donnelly, was renamed the Donnelly Memorial Theater.

Chapter 3

The Donnelly Theater

A priest who was fresh off a battleship attempted to run the Donnelly Theater in which we began to perform in the fall of 1959. He had the floors painted gray, in a shipshape way. Father Quirk (whose nickname quickly became for us, Father Queeg) had difficulty understanding that theater people could not conform to business hours of nine to five. Sometimes it was necessary to rehearse all night because stagehands had to be doing things on the stage while the cast was sleeping. Negotiating with him about the use of the theater was a constant hassle.

While preparations were being made for a visit from the cardinal we were bemused to see a scarlet curtain go up in front of the stage of the theater. As we anticipated, when the cardinal came to show off the theater and stepped in front of the curtain all of him disappeared except his face and his hands.

For our production of Italian composer Luigi Nono's *Intolleranza*, a contemporary opera highlighting intolerance in its many guises, we had a very different kind of curtain. During a research trip I made to Prague with Nono, we met with Jozef Svoboda, a master set designer who was Czech. He demonstrated his light curtain for us. Basically it was a long row of lights that were projected down while water was sprayed in the air, creating a curtain through which a person could walk and disappear. The only obstacle to vision was the light.

The best directors participate to an enormous extent in deciding how lighting will be used. What lighting can do is help shift the audience's attention continually. There are laws that determine where you look on the stage and I always have to be conscious of this and work with them. If I do not, they work against me. Directing the audience's eye from one thing to another is the way I tell a story. If lights come up over there, you are going to look over there. If something drops over here, your eyes will look here.

If I am an actor on the stage and I look in a certain direction the audience will turn to see what I'm looking at. The craft of using these laws to make the audience watch what *you* want them to watch works because it is important to control the sequence of impressions. Sometimes these impressions come through the text, sometimes they come through the music, and sometimes they come through watching an actor's face react to the situation.

When we use slides and projections, a professional lighting designer has to make them work with the lighting. He knows what equipment is needed, and there is a lot of experimentation. In one hall because of the way the lights are hung and focused you may need less equipment than in another hall. The light must not spill over the proscenium where the text is projected.

One of the great directors is Giorgio Strehler who works in Italy. He uses a wonderfully simple system. He does the lighting first. The lights are set on the stage and each actor is instructed where to sit and to move to make best use of the lighting for the desired visual effects, such as light crossing his face, or resting on his shoulders.

When Jozef Svoboda had earlier brought his magic curtain (from his Laterna Magika Theatre) to Carnegie Hall, I was eager to talk with him about the possibility of working with us on a production in Boston. I was able to find out when his boxes were to be unpacked. At about midnight on a spring night I went to a space behind Carnegie Hall. When a big wooden box was placed on the sidewalk, I of course was eager to know what kind of magical equipment was inside. A workman opened it and I saw that it was full of toilet paper. This was amusing because at that time

Americans were warned to take toilet paper when they traveled to Europe. Obviously the Czechs had been told that they should bring toilet paper to America. Perhaps they thought that it would be hard to find or that it would be prohibitively expensive. Svoboda agreed to come to Boston to design our production of *Intolleranza*. In addition to the light curtain he made a series of screens in various shapes and dimensions that were covered in black velour and hung in the air. Because the background was also black velour they were both there and not there. They opened mechanically by remote control in different ways, some like the iris of a lens of a camera, while others had shutter openings. Focused on these screens were projectors that, making use of closed-circuit television, made it possible to project either informational or affectively emotional slides. Other cameras photographed details of what was on the stage and projected them, enormously blown up, on the screens.

The events to be presented were placed in sequence on the screens to enhance the development of the plot. It centered on the tragic consequences of people everywhere misunderstanding each other.

After being rejected by Woman, who misunderstands his homesickness, Man, a miner who yearns for the homeland from which he is a refugee, is caught up by mistake in a political demonstration. He is sent to a prison camp where, despite dreadful physical conditions, he finds love and humanity. In the end the world is flooded to make way for a new beginning. The opera highlights the necessity for tolerance and cooperation in an imperfect world.

In Prague, Luigi Nono and I had met with Czech costume designer Jan Skalický. Nono was very excited about the idea that Skalický would do the costumes, but when he came to America for the production, he disliked what Skalický had done. It was his first western exposure, therefore he had everything made at couturier shops in Prague. Included were a collection of stunning hand-knit sweaters; and impeccably tailored men's clothing. Although we got the costumes at a great bargain, because they were so carefully made, enormous duty was demanded by U.S. Customs.

Because Nono objected to the costumes we decided not to buy them but to rent them for a short time and return them to Europe as used clothing. I contacted a young theater student whom I knew in Germany and offered to sell everything to him for one dollar. We shipped the clothing to Hamburg where he collected it and distributed it to impoverished students and actors in Berlin who enjoyed an unexpected warm and colorful winter.

What Nono was after, I soon realized, was for actors to wear their own old clothes, well-worn jeans, sweaters, and jackets. He disliked the designer look. He disliked even more costumes designed for a scene in a concentration camp. Skalický had created simple striped smocks to make the cast look like prisoners. They were to be put in groups and wrapped in barbed wire. I considered this effective and appropriate costuming.

The concentration camp consisted of what looked like two pieces of barbed wire. Actually it was two light boxes, very long, about twenty or thirty feet, one vertical and one horizontal, and cut out to appear as barbed wire. When they were lit there appeared to be a barbed wire of light. It did not occur to anyone except Nono, who was an Italian Communist, that it looked like a cross. When he came to the theater and saw it, he went shouting down the aisle that it was a cheap trick to make his play appear to be Christian.

Although the Russian electrician from Boston University and Svoboda claimed to understand each other perfectly, they did not. The result was that slides were put improperly in boxes and, as a result, cracked. Appearing unexpectedly one day when dummy slides were being projected to make sure the system worked correctly, Nono became incensed and abusive about how we were trying to make a mockery of his opera.

Because the Communist Czech government collected most of the money that was earned by the performing artists they allowed to travel overseas, Jozef Svoboda and his assistant cooked hot dogs in his room so he could save the dollars he was allowed to keep. It did not surprise us when Jan Skalický decided to remain in America to work.

In contrast to working with the Czechs, dealing with Luigi Nono was a challenge. I was fascinated with trying to find out how his mind worked, what he was trying to get at. I was intrigued by the concept of his theatrical vision and I very much wanted to find out what it was. Rather than fight with him, which maybe I should have done, I think in retrospect that as artistic director if I had taken a stand on certain things that I thought were great, the production would have been more successful. We did very much let him have what he wanted.

By the time Luigi Nono arrived in Boston he was wildly irritated and his behavior while he remained in Boston indicated this in many ways. Getting him to Boston in 1965 was difficult. In supporting his visa we encountered a law that stated that although Communists from Communist countries could come to the United States, Communists from non-Communist countries were barred from admission to our country. Before a last-minute exception was made to enable him to come, he sent letters to members of the Boston Symphony beginning, "Dear Comrade! I know that you will serve my opera well even though I cannot come myself. . . ."

He got to Boston together with his wife and small children two or three days before the date for which the opening performance, an American premiere, had been announced. Because of the changes he insisted upon, and the late arrival of the conductor, Bruno Maderna, the opening had to be postponed.

Time magazine and *Life* magazine, both of which had opened their archives so we could find photographs of incidents of intolerance worldwide, followed the production closely and publicized the details.

When Nono first got to Boston he escaped from us. Literally, he ran away; we couldn't find him for a while. When he reappeared it was during a rehearsal. He came into the theater, screaming, "It's a cheap capitalist trick! It's a lie!!" and the reporters were there to hear him.

"What, Luigi," I asked, "is a cheap capitalist lie?" His answer was that not all students who went to Harvard University were Communist. He was deadly serious. He had managed to get to Harvard and contact a Communist cell but he could find only five or six people there and he was frustrated.

The presentation of *Intolleranza* in Boston was an event almost as newsworthy as the world premiere five years earlier in 1960 in Venice, when the opera had been the object of a demonstration by a Fascist group. Although it had innovative and extraordinary visual and musical effects, I think the hullabaloo in Boston was caused mainly by the fact that the press focused so much attention on it.

Nono made himself so unpopular in Boston that his activity was the subject of a television interview during a televised version of *Intolleranza* (televised because it had been supported in part by public funds). Participating were the president of our opera company, Laszlo Bonis, *Boston Globe* critic Michael Steinberg, and Beverly Sills, who sang the female lead.

I opted not to take part because I felt that in some way he had been "had." I became annoyed by people who thought I was a Communist dupe because I believed what was being said in the opera. There was nothing in the content that I had not been taught by the Methodist church. The purpose of the interview was to criticize, ridicule, and strike back at Nono.

I did find it sad and ironic that Luigi Nono, having created an opera excoriating intolerance, exhibited himself to be so intolerant personally. Not only Boston and Harvard disappointed Luigi Nono. His mother-in-law, a nifty lady, Gertrude Schoenberg (the widow of composer Arnold Schoenberg), who had come to Boston to help see that all went well, reported after Nono came to visit her in California that he didn't trust her any more because she wouldn't show him slums as bad as he was sure were there. She said he went on to the Soviet Union to remonstrate with the Soviets because his music was banned there. From Moscow he telephoned her to say that it was dreadful there, that his music was misunderstood, and that he was on his way to Cuba.

Whether *Intolleranza* affected our fund-raising attempts we'll never know. Presumably people who supported our efforts to present contemporary opera that centered on social concerns were not put off by the public spectacle of Nono's presence in Boston. Because of it we may have lost some support, but it was never difficult to sell tickets to our productions.

We tried different techniques for fund-raising, since of necessity it remained at the forefront of our consciousness. Once our reputation as a first-rate opera company was established, we found that mailings worked very well. People were generous in their contributions because they felt that the work we were doing was exciting and meaningful.

In 1965 we were fortunate in having Joan Sutherland, the Australian soprano who had performed the role of Semiramide in Rossini's opera at La Scala, come to Boston and sing it for us. The "trouser" role of Arsace, the young man to whom Semiramide, the Queen of Babylon, is attracted (and who turns out to be her son) was sung by Marilyn Horne, a mezzo-soprano who was well-known enough to help us sell tickets. She filled her trouser role well, since she happened to be pregnant.

Prince Assur, who has helped Semiramide murder her husband, expects to become king but he is forestalled by the ghost of King Ninus, who proclaims that Arsace will be his successor. Arsace, trying to stab his rival, stabs, instead, Semiramide, who comes between them.

The scene that the audience remembered best was when Semiramide made her entrance in a chariot carried by "the people." She almost missed her cue because she was having so much fun backstage releasing doves to fly about the stage.

Joan Sutherland liked the costumes that our designer made for her so much that she continued to order costumes from him. Recently she sold them in an auction.

Marilyn Horne returned a few seasons later to sing the title role in *Carmen*. We were to open in Boston, then move to California for another performance. She insisted that her husband, Henry Lewis, conduct. Although her voice was good, I wanted her to act the part as well. As she was not naturally graceful, I hired a flamenco dancer to give her lessons in how to move in the role of Carmen. While she was trying to learn, her husband sat and laughed at her.

It became an impossible situation when he was rude and sarcastic to the orchestra. I was shocked. In fact, the orchestra said it would not perform if he directed. I told him that he couldn't treat musicians that way and that he would have to apologize.

His retort was, "If you fire me, Marilyn won't sing."

I said, "Marilyn has a contract. I would much rather have it turn out pleasant and well. I'd rather have you apologize to the orchestra."

He did apologize, and was civil from then on, presumably because they didn't want to lose the money, and our *Carmen* went to California. I was not surprised to hear that their marriage didn't last.

We formed opera guilds to help us with publicity and fundraising by organizing several teas all in one day. Ladies in several suburban areas gave teas and invited their friends. I made a recording that enabled me to speak to all of them. We distributed printed materials. Suddenly we had a big guild that helped provide financial support.

Keeping in mind that our purpose is to entertain as well as to educate, I always reserve the right to determine the way money is spent. I do this on the simple theory that there will never be enough to do everything we would like to do. Of course, there are certain things on which we have to spend money. I never hire singers unless I can hear them in a big hall. I rent a hall if I am in

New York, at Juilliard, at the Mannes School or sometimes the Little Carnegie Hall where I audition all day. In Boston I audition in the hall where we will be performing.

We know what the minimum cost for the orchestra and for the chorus will be. When we actually start working with the production, we have the singers under contract and we know that 80 percent of the budget is set. That's not where it is easy to go wrong. It's the last 20 percent that can suddenly become forty or fifty percent of the total if we are not extremely careful. How we spend that money is what is most important.

We can seldom have all the orchestra rehearsal time we want, or have the ideal costumes made, or have as much lighting rehearsal time as we need, or find certain props we would like to use. We have a specific amount of money and when we get close to the opening date for the performance, every expenditure becomes an artistic decision. It is always, "Do I hire a second oboe, have another hour's overtime with the strings, or rent three extra lights?" It is constantly necessary to try to determine what is most important.

One of the large costs for a new production is set design. Before approaching the set designers I decide what I think will work and places where problems might appear. I determine what the basic sequence of events in the performance will be and decide how best to show them. I work with the designers and tell them what we need and they come back with some models and their ideas. We discuss back and forth until we come to something I am convinced will work. With collaboration, often we don't remember which ideas were whose.

Set designers get paid to design. The cost of the sets is not their problem. Sometimes they have nothing to do with building the set. Sometimes they prefer to do it all. When we have a model of the set we take it to several different scene shops, usually to New York, or Boston, or to New Jersey, or to Israel (which has one of the better scene shops) for estimates of the cost of building the set. When the estimate comes back it is invariably much more than we can possibly afford so I return to the set designers and often ask them to redesign it so it can be built for half the cost.

It's far more complicated if the scenic designer, the costume designer, and the lighting designer are different people because they all work in different ways, and the more people you have working on a production the more difficult collaboration becomes. Our production of Arnold Schoenberg's *Moses und Aron*, for example, required extremely close cooperation on the part of everyone from beginning to end.

The Donnelly Theater where we were performing had good acoustics, and quite good sight lines. The stage was much too small but as we did one opera at a time we could find ways to make the disadvantages work for us. We built a ramp out around the orchestra pit. We built stairs from the stage to the ramp, providing massive areas for activity. We used boxes that were quite high on either side of the stage for part of the set, creating places to which the cast could go that they could not have reached on a conventional stage.

Moses und Aron, by Arnold Schoenberg, is one of the great works of our time. It is first and foremost a choral opera. The president of the Handel and Haydn Society, an old Boston institution, and I went to London to see the Covent Garden performance at Gertrude Schoenberg's suggestion. It was a beautiful production.

She was considering letting us perform the American premiere of her late husband's opera because when she was in Boston with her son-in-law, Luigi Nono, she had seen how hard we worked, and how seriously and well we did *Intolleranza*. She didn't give her permission in London, though.

She said, "I'm going to Berlin for my birthday and if you want to come to Berlin I'll try to make up my mind then."

John Cunningham, our manager, was with me. We went to Berlin. When we got there we were told we could not see Gertrude Schoenberg for two days.

John had some friends in Berlin with whom he went partying and celebrated too much. While he was recovering I had a call from Gertrude Schoenberg. She wanted to come right over. I called John and asked him to join us. He got all dressed up and tried very hard to appear sober. He was very nervous.

It was her birthday. It was also Sunday and the hotel was not equipped for much. Nevertheless, John managed to find two dozen roses and a cake that said "Happy Birthday." When she arrived, she announced, "I'm hungry. I want some steak!"

John went to the end of the lobby where he thought he arranged for a dozen miniature roast beef hors d'oeuvres but they turned out to be quite large open-faced steak sandwiches. He returned, and holding a bottle of champagne, sang in a cracked voice, "Happy Birthday, Dear Gertrude!" She wanted more champagne, then more champagne. It turned into a very expensive evening.

She did agree, though, to let us do the production. Then came the problem of who would conduct. Arnold Schoenberg's life in California, where he had very little money and for that reason trouble making ends meet, had been miserable. He was bitter about his treatment from publishers and performers. Because of this I assured Gertrude Schoenberg that we would have a conductor of whom she approved.

Back home again, I got a series of telephone calls, usually at midnight or at three o'clock in the morning, depending on from where she was calling. The conversation would be something like this, "Sarah, it cannot be such and such a person. He did something dreadful to my husband." We went through practically every conductor known to the profession. It seemed everybody had someway done something not to help her husband. Most of it, I was sure, was imaginary.

Then came Pierre Boulez. She said, "Now I want you to call Boulez. I want Boulez to do it." So I got Boulez's phone number; we found him in Scotland, as I recall. I talked to him and he said, "No, I don't want to conduct this piece. I don't like the piece. I don't want to do it." I said, "Look, Mrs. Schoenberg is eager for you to do it. We can fit the production date to fit your schedule." "No. No. No!" he said, "Don't bother me again!" and he hung up.

I thought I couldn't tell Gertrude Schoenberg this but I did call her to say I had talked to Boulez and he was terribly busy and was so sorry he couldn't do it. Well, Mrs. Schoenberg claimed she called Boulez herself and that he swore that I had not talked to him. I got so mad I told her all the things he said. Then I suggested, "Let's make a conference call together. Let's both call Boulez." Then she believed me.

Meanwhile Osbourne McConathy in Boston had been conducting and training the chorus and making the choir sound absolutely wonderful. They knew the piece, which is 98 percent choral, inside out. He also had been preparing the orchestra parts from a photostat of the original manuscript. His responsibility was to make sure that when we got to the first orchestra rehearsal the parts would be in as good order. He said that the best way to save money would be for him to have individual rehearsals with members of the orchestra. He learned *Moses und Aron* better than anybody ever had.

At the same time, Mrs. Schoenberg was still working over a list of her late husband's perceived enemies. One thing Osbourne McConathy was not was an enemy, as he had never met Schoenberg. It was never his intention to conduct *Moses und Aron* but in the end, he did it, beautifully.

In Covent Garden there was an enormous stage and you were quite far from the stage when you sat in the audience. There was a sacrificial scene in which they had live goats that were carried across the stage. This was very effective. I contacted Theatrical Animals, Inc. because I thought using animals was a dramatic effect that I would like to use in our production.

I didn't consider where we would keep the animals. I assumed, I suppose, that they would stay in the truck. But they had to get into the theater somehow. In building a ramp around the orchestra pit we had made what was really a cattle run. It was covered but open. When the animals arrived, I was not in the theater. The trainers saw the pen and thought it had been constructed for the sheep, so they put them inside. When I came into the theater to attend a rehearsal, the orchestra was all abuzz and the ramp was full of smelly sheep and goats stamping their little feet and going "Baaa."

Now McConathy was understandably nervous about this whole operation. When he came for the rehearsal, it was absolutely too late to do anything about it, so he acted as if the sheep and goats were not there.

Meanwhile a state veterinarian came. It was amazing how many people had to be talked to and how many licenses had to be gotten before we could get permission to use live animals onstage. One of the things we were trying to do was determine how much sedative to give each of these little animals so it could be carried across the stage without going wild and perhaps escaping into the audience.

The veterinarian set up shop in the back of the theater and during the orchestra rehearsal he sedated the animals. Every time he did it there would be this horrible agonized screech from an animal being stuck. He obviously didn't have a technique for doing it painlessly. No matter where we were in the rehearsal, because we had to solve this problem, an actor would walk across the stage carrying this little body with its tongue lolling out.

The rehearsal was finished and McConathy left. I was amazed by how he comported himself because for him ordinarily any distraction from the concentration of an orchestra rehearsal was a major sin.

I talked to the animal trainer and said, "Obviously this is not going to work. Our theater is too small." He agreed, and the animals were loaded back into their truck and they departed.

At three o'clock in the morning my phone rang. It was McConathy. He didn't sound emotional or upset. Instead he was cold and controlled. He said, "Sarah, I have had a meeting with my family, with my children and my wife," and I thought, "Oops! Where do we go from here?" He said, "I don't approve of ultimatums, as you know. However, reluctantly, I must say, 'Either the animals go or I go!'"

I burst out laughing and that made him furious. I said, "Ozzie, I have to tell you that great minds are in the same channel. The animals by now have reached New Jersey." When he said he didn't believe it, I got serious and explained, "Obviously it was impossible to use live animals and I apologize for what happened at the rehearsal. I thought you were a saint to put up with all of that. It was clear that we couldn't use the animals so I sent them home." The next day after I called to make sure they had gotten there safely, they sent a telegram to Ozzie.

For the presentation, set designer Oliver Smith, and I decided to take a totally different point of view. The back wall would be painted gold. There would be no props of any kind. I knew a very talented Israeli mime, Claude Kipnes, who had worked in Paris with Marcel Marceau. I engaged him to help us. We went to nothing. Everything was imaginary, including the staffs of Moses and Aron. It was very effective.

We had announced the production for the spring but we couldn't present it because the chorus was the main thing and it was not ready. I had hired a famous chorusmeister, a lady from Chicago who ran all the Chicago Symphony choruses. She came to Boston. She went to several universities, and talked with choral departments and with our own chorus, and the Handel and Haydn Chorus made up a schedule. The amount of money we were paying that lady, just in transportation alone, was unbelievable.

The choruses were supposed to be ready by a specific date in April. Two weeks before that date I received a letter from her saying it just wasn't working. She presumably had been coaching the groups for three months. I asked her to bring the choruses together; I wanted to hear them. Certain groups were angry because she had not come to some of their scheduled rehearsals. So I fired her.

We postponed the production until November. That gave us time to audition and put together a volunteer and professional chorus.

Because of the mime movements you would swear that Moses, the inarticulate one, and Aron, the articulate one, had staffs. You didn't quite realize they didn't until all of a sudden you did. The audience loved it. It was different.

The music was extraordinary and beautiful. McConathy worked five nights a week all summer long with the chorus. They sang as if it were really quite simple music—which it wasn't. It was a difficult work that made a very big impression.

Mrs. Schoenberg, unfortunately, was not able to attend the opening because she became sick.

Chapter 4

The Back Bay Theater

When the Donnelly Theater was sold by the Catholics to the Christian Scientists in 1966, it became once again the Back Bay Theater (which most people had called it all along). Our performance there of Modest Musorgsky's opera, *Boris Godunov*, about events in early seventeenth-century Russia, using Musorgsky's original orchestration, was the first American performance of the original version.

We performed the music as it was written before it was rejected, in 1870, by the St. Petersburg Orchestra. It was the music as it was written before the scene on the Lithuanian border was inserted. It was the music composed before the part of Marina was added because it was assumed that to be accepted in St. Petersburg an opera must have a heroine. It was also before Boris, not the suffering Russian masses, became the focus of the opera.

The thing that happened to Musorgsky was that his friends who were composers "improved" almost everything he wrote. The version of *Boris Godunov* we heard up to the time we did it in Boston had been redone by Rimsky-Korsakov. Since that time there have been several performances of what was purported to be the original Musorgsky opera but when editors got hold of it the desire to improve, and to change, was so great that when the Metropolitan first did anything with Musorgsky's orchestration, it had many changes in it.

It was difficult to get the music. We had announced that we were going to do the original version of *Boris Godunov* before I went to England to get the scores. When I got to England, they said I couldn't have them because there was only one set. I tried using contacts in the Soviet Union but my requests went unanswered. It was a scary time. I learned not to announce performances until we had the music in hand.

Finally, with the help of Walter Felsenstein, the legendary Intendant at the Komische Oper in East Berlin, I went to the larger opera company in East Berlin. They had scores that had been made by their copyist while working with a young Russian musicologist whose task was to check and make sure that the orchestra parts corresponded with the original manuscript. There had been no playing around with it and nobody had used it. We were able to have copies made for ourselves. We found that everything Musorgsky had written originally in *Boris Godunov* was quite playable. There were sounds that one didn't hear in the ornamented versions of his music.

I had good support in Boston from a dear friend, Olga Pertzoff, and her family. Her uncle had been one of the first envoys to Russia, and her husband, Constantine, had escaped as a very young man at the time of the revolution under a heap of furs in a sleigh.

In order to get Rudolph Heinrich to design the set and the costumes I visited him in Hannover, Germany. He insisted he didn't have the time. We had lunch together and while we were discussing the opera, he began to make sketches at the lunch table and that did it; he agreed to be our designer.

Those sketches were not a bit traditional. There are a lot of scenes in *Boris Godunov* and we wanted to be able to get from scene to scene without stopping if we could. What Rudolph designed was a three-tiered stage. At the top there was a series of very beautiful icons. It was the religious level. On the second level were deeply carved, simple, barbaric gold panels.

On this platform everything that had to do with royalty took place. Then there were stairs that could be descended to floor level. On the floor level the set was built on scaffolding. There were doors that opened from above and there were pieces that covered the lower level that flew down from the top. The effect was rustic and peasantlike. The lower level also became the monastery, with three dark cells far below the lighted icons on the upper level.

For *Boris Godunov* I was, as almost always, both conductor and stage director. I find the most valuable thing for me as the director is to pretend I am in the theater for the first time and sit in a chair as if I know nothing at all about what is going to happen. The curtain goes up and I have a variety of experiences. I observe things. I see a very interesting set or I don't like any of it. I think, "Where did they get that chair? Isn't it wonderful?" or, "How awful it is!"

The way scenery is constructed has a lot to do with the acoustical results. I hear music and things start to happen. I listen and I react. As the director I try to sit as long as I can and always come back to that chair, and try to weigh the experiences the audience is having. If I want the audience to look at someone and then I want them to look away, in the simplest terms, I can have a loud noise—the sound of gun fire, for example—giving some reason to look toward a certain place. I can have a performer look in a certain direction and the audience will look in that direction also because everyone is curious to see what he's looking at. None of these things are terribly profound but they work.

Lights can be changed and all of a sudden you can't see. When there's a bright light, you turn to look at it. A door opens. Any change attracts attention. These are just natural laws, laws in terms of the fact that they will produce reactions that I, the director, can then control.

Movement on the stage should be related to where the focus of attention should be. What you see on the stage, the physical form of what happens, needs also to relate to what is in the music. The director's problem in something episodic is to clarify the line that is followed through the whole thing.

The technique that seems to work best is that one operates on the theory that the composer imagined a scenario, a series of events, and wrote music for it. It is not true that all composers had dramatic ideas that they then wrote music for, but it is true that for hearing and seeing on the stage it is helpful to make this assumption.

I think the movement of the idea should come a fraction of a section before the music, rather than allowing the music to indicate change. As stage director my job is to figure out a dramatic reason for each change in the music. Then the music will function well. The composer may have operated with a different theory. He may have written the music as part of a musical form, but I must structure it in the playing, in my presentation of the action, so it has also a dramatic form. When it works together it's good. If it doesn't work together then the audience doesn't know what's the matter, but something isn't quite right, and the attention of the audience begins to wander.

Acting as the conductor, before staging a choral scene—and *Boris Godunov* had several very important ones—I have people go for an hour to different positions for different parts of the chorus: tenors *here*, for example, and basses *there*. We try different positions to get the best music for the particular music and the particular set.

Once I know where to get the best sound, I try to group and motivate people and invent reasons for them, to go to these places with what seems comfortable and natural behavior, so the music will sound the best it can. In doing that, quite often I discover places where the sound is not so good as it could be. To alleviate this we have little speakers placed in the set that take the sound of the orchestra to the stage. The singers control the volume of those little speakers. There might be a table on which there are some books and hidden in those books is a tiny speaker. There can be two or more places where the singers can go to turn the volume up or down depending on what they need. If the singer is writing a letter she can turn the sound up a bit and when she has finished she can turn it down. It is the simplest possible kind of a system and has solved a myriad of problems.

The balance of sound all over the house is different. It is the conductor's job to regulate the dynamic values so that you don't drown people out, you don't play so softly that the music can't be heard; and you must manage to get a dynamic variation so you can change from the softest to the loudest to make an exciting effect.

Success can be determined in split seconds, determined by how the conductor turns a phrase, or defines the moment something new begins. In a relationship between beginnings and endings and musical forms, a clarity must exist between phrases from which the listener gets the impression of newness, of freshness, and of endings and beginnings.

Our Boris was George London, the Canadian bass-baritone who, having studied in the United States, became the first non-Russian to sing the part of Boris in Moscow.

The most dramatic visual part of the opera came during the coronation scene, which was full of beautiful banners and gorgeous icons that the Russian community of Boston had worked with Heinrich to create. The coronation scene was a continuous moving thing. While bells tolled, Boris moved from the level with richly dressed nobles and beautiful banners to the upper level and then came down to the level of the peasants. When he left the stage we went to black, and when the lights came up in the center of the stage platform there was an enormous staircase covered with brilliant red carpeting. At the top was a throne.

At the end of the coronation ceremony Boris walked up the stairs where there was a priest, and a little boy. They handed him the symbols of power: the robe, the scepter, and the crown. He turned and that was it. It was a wonderfully dramatic scene.

The priest in this scene was Mr. Haffenreffer, and the little boy was his son, Hughey. When Hugh grew up, he became a Lutheran minister.

At the end of the opera Boris crumpled in delirium at the top of the stairs and rolled down.

A year later we produced *Boris Godunov* again. When I went to Rome to see Boris Christoff, the Bulgarian bass internationally famous for interpreting the role, to ask him to come and sing in Boston, I took with me a model of the set that we had used. I didn't want to have any trouble when he came and saw that it was very different from the sets to which he was accustomed. He professed to think it was the most wonderful set he had seen, a very exciting concept, he thought.

Two weeks later he fell, hit his head, and had an aneurism that required a brain operation. It was successful. This was about eight months before he was to come to Boston. He came when he was expected. He told me about the terrible thing that had happened to him and confessed, "I'm terrified I will forget but I want to do what you ask me to do." I said, "We'll do absolutely whatever you want." His request was that we change the set to make it more like the one to which he was accustomed.

Because making such changes destroyed the concept of our visual presentation of the opera, there were people who felt that I should not have given in to Christoff's request that the set be changed. Perhaps they were right, but I believed him when he said that he was terrified to do it differently.

We did nevertheless hear Boris Christoff's magnificent voice and the superb chorus that had worked so hard together with the musicians to produce an opera that reverberates in memory decades later.

Soon after Boris Christoff performed with us in *Boris Godunov*, in early April 1966, we presented *Hippolyte et Aricie*, an opera by Jean-Philippe Rameau that had first been performed in 1733 in Paris, where it was spurned by the critics and adored by the public.

Ours was the first fully staged performance of the opera in the United States. It was based by Rameau and his librettist, the Abbé Pellegrin, on Racine's *Phèdre* after Euripides' classic drama concerning suspected incest, jealousy, and love. Phèdre, the wife of Thésée, falls in love with her stepson, Hippolyte. Thésée, assuming that Hippolyte has assaulted his stepmother, banishes him. While trying to escape from Phèdre so he can be with his lover, Aricie, Hippolyte is killed by a sea monster and Phèdre kills herself.

Rameau was criticized for changing the emphasis from Phèdre, the stepmother, to Aricie. In our production, Beverly Sills was Aricie and a little-known but very talented Plácido Domingo was Hippolyte.

Music publishing has varied through the years in terms of what publishers consider appropriate. In Rameau's time the tune for the singer and the words were printed and the bass line was indicated but none of the intermediary music was included. More that two hundred years after that first performance, the only published score we could find was one that had only the top and the bottom. Many years after Rameau's death, Camille Saint-Saëns made a version in which he used nineteenth-century church organists' harmony, which falsified the clarity. That was not the version we wanted.

As Rameau himself had conducted the opera, I was sure that somewhere there were orchestra parts. If we had those orchestra parts, we could write it all out and we would know what it was harmonically.

While I was in Paris with our business manager, John Cunningham, we went to the Paris Opera Library, which houses music from various operatic theaters. The most remarkable thing about the Paris Opera Library is that it was to a very great extent uncatalogued. They assured us that they did not have the music for which we were searching.

John Cunningham found a maiden lady there whom he romanced. He brought her flowers; he brought her a bottle of wine; he took her to lunch. My part was to look dour and storm out and appear to be jealous. After about three or four days John was allowed to go into the stacks, which were closed to the public. He went back and forth for about a week and finally came back with a rather large folder wrapped in cream-colored paper. It contained the orchestra parts of *Hippolyte and Aricie.* This score was presumably the one used for the performance as conducted by Rameau.

John got it photostatted and we brought it back to America. Osbourne McConathy took those parts, as well as everything we could find by Rameau, including scores different people had written in pencil—even notations about the singers. From that material Ozzie made a score that made it possible for the orchestra, which he conducted, to perform with the proper harmonies.

Herbert Senn and Helen Pond did the sets in the style of the period, of which we had photographs of many paintings and pictures. Rameau wrote the opera when architectural books had instructions on how to turn the ballroom of your castle into an opera house or a theater. It was a stylized kind of presentation.

One of the great moments is when Hippolyte is followed on the stage by a sea monster. The creature was enormous. We saw only the front part of him. Hippolyte was fighting him and the monster would drive him back. Hippolyte would back up and engage the monster, which had many tentacles. Finally the sea monster grabbed his sword and pulled Hippolyte until finally there was a moment when he flew. I've forgotten how we did it; it took a lot of work, but his legs went up and he was suddenly in the jaws of the thing. It was so scary and unexpected that nobody laughed. In the end Hippolyte is resurrected and reunited with Aricie.

The following season, in February 1967, we produced Mozart's *Don Giovanni.* The set was designed by Oliver Smith, a brilliant designer for the ballet theater, also well known for having designed sets for Lerner and Loewe's *My Fair Lady.* He was a close friend of Mrs. Jacqueline Kennedy. He liked what we were doing, so he invited her to Boston to attend some of the rehearsals. She brought with her to the opening the French minister of culture, André Malraux, and his wife.

In order to show that Don Giovanni's house was decadent and odd, we engaged some little people, that is, midgets, and they were the servants. Giovanni, sung by Robert Dooley, had three dogs, the kind of dogs that have no voices, tall, thin, very elegant dogs.

There is a moment when Zerlina is raped by Don Giovanni. We had scenery that revolved. In one on the floor there were animal rugs. The dogs were there, and Giovanni was there, and as the revolving stage came into the light, Giovanni grabbed Zerlina and forced her down on the rug. It was altogether sick and wonderful and in rehearsal it worked very well. At the opening performance the dogs went wild. They broke away from the dwarfs and they attacked Giovanni. Fortunately, the dog trainer who was on the side of the stage, came running out, got the dogs, and dragged them away, and we finished the act. It made the papers; in fact, it got quite a bit of play. The combination of midgets and dogs and rape was quite something for a Boston audience to experience.

Mrs. Kennedy agreed to be honorary chairman of a fund-raising party, a masked ball, which we planned to hold the following January. There was great excitement in preparing for that event as Mrs. Kennedy was expected to attend. In the end, she did not come because she injured her finger in a riding accident.

We began our next drive for funds with a less formal evening, which we called "A Night in Old Vienna." For a hundred dollars, people bought tickets to attend a rathskeller buffet with dancing and to meet the guest of honor, my mother's special friend, Kitty Carlisle.

A lot of the life of the Opera Company of Boston—nine years—took place in the Donnelly–Back Bay Theater where we staged forty-five productions. After it was bought by the Christian Scientists, they threatened and threatened to tear it down, but eventually agreed to delay its destruction for a year, at our request. Their explanation was that the building was in poor repair, did not have air-conditioning, and was not being used 82 percent of the time.

One of our last performances at the Back Bay was Humper-dinck's *Hänsel and Gretel.* It was our tradition to present *Hänsel and Gretel* during each Christmas season. Adults were invited to attend only if they were accompanied by children. For every perfor-mance, before the opera began, the conductor came out and re-hearsed the children in the music that they would hear when the children who had been turned into cookies would wake up at the end of the opera.

After the music was played, the children were transformed into gingerbread cookies. At the end of the opera, *Hänsel and Gretel* danced out into the audience, turned the gingerbread boys and girls back into children and tossed them candy. Twenty or thirty were invited up on the stage to surround the gingerbread house, which was covered with candy (carefully wrapped so the children wouldn't get germs). After it was over, they could stay to eat the witch's house, which was made of gingerbread and had sixty pounds of sugar icing for decoration.

Over the years we had different sets for *Hänsel and Gretel* but the participation of the children remained the same. In one produc-tion, the set was hidden behind an enormous broom, the house rolled forward, and the furniture danced.

One sad day the Back Bay Theater was demolished to make way for a multistory apartment building with a parking garage and stores. Once again the Opera Company was homeless.

Chapter 5

The Shubert Theater

We rented the Shubert, a small theater that held fewer than half the people we were accustomed to seating at the Back Bay. The Shubert was a Broadway try-out theater with a nice stage; it looked like a Broadway house but the seats were packed together so tightly that people's knees got squeezed.

There I directed and conducted Donizetti's *Lucia di Lammermoor*. Herbert Senn and Helen Pond, the two marvelous designers and dear friends with whom I had worked on many operas, went along with me to Italy and Scotland on research trips.

I was fascinated by the fact that *Lucia* is an opera that deals with the nature of madness. It is based on a book written by Sir Walter Scott, a writer who suffered from madness. He had terrible attacks and splitting wild headaches. When he felt an attack coming on, he would send everyone in the house away and he would be all alone with his dog. His neighbors would hear him howling and the dog howling and it was a very frightening thing.

As a child I believed that Sir Walter Scott was in our family because there was a man named Mr. Scott, and his first name was Walter, whom my grandmother's grandmother had married. I heard great funny stories of Mr. Scott, who was not much liked by the rest of the family. According to family legend, my grandmother's mother remarried quite late in life. She lived in Kansas City and owned a great deal of property, including a beautiful house overlooking the river, and a great deal of land, which included several blocks of what is now downtown Kansas City.

When Mr. Scott died, the family lawyer was said to have been entrusted in Walter Scott's will with the task of taking certain documents and burning them and taking other documents and burying them with him. I suspect he was given this job, because he was, I wouldn't say the *only* honest member of the family, but certainly the only one who would have done it without reading the papers.

When I was young, I knew about the legend in our family, and I thought it was true. I believed it when I heard that deeds to much of seven or eight blocks of downtown Kansas City, prime property where large buildings were standing, were in question because this had been the property of an elderly lady who left no instructions about what should happen to it.

There were those of us, and I belonged to that small contingent, who wanted very much to get a court order to dig up Mr. Scott, who was buried in Kansas City, and see what was buried with him.

I still think it was ridiculous we didn't, to see if the deeds had actually been put there to spite the family that had been monstrously unpleasant to him. Because he outlived my great-great-grandmother, he inherited everything, and the rest of the family received nothing.

I heard these stories as a very little child and at the same time heard of Sir Walter Scott, so it's not surprising that the two people got confused in my mind. For a long time I believed that Sir Walter Scott was in my family, and that he was a really unpleasant man.

Donizetti, the composer himself, also died ravished by the effects of madness. In quite early life he began to have dreadful headaches and later became preoccupied with the manifestation of insanity and madness.

We went to Bergamo, which was his home. It is a charming little town in Italy, a couple of hours' drive outside of Milan, in a landscape that made us feel we were in a painting. In Bergamo, we went to the bookstores and to the shops to buy everything that we could find that was written about Donizetti. There was a lot: I found six fascinating books that remain part of my library.

We got permission to go to the Donizetti Museum. Not many people in those days visited that museum. In the museum there were hundreds of photographs and manuscripts and under glass was the black morning coat that Donizetti was buried in. It was full of worm holes. And in another case under glass was his skull. They dug him up because they wanted to try to study his head, and perhaps other parts of his remains, to see if they could determine what form of madness caused him to have those terrible terrible spells.

As Sir Walter Scott had done quite a lot of writing about his own madness, so did Donizetti about his.

We had two cameras and took many pictures. We thought we might use photographic details of the house in the course of the production of *Lucia di Lammermoor.* We had a concept of mixing in slides to illustrate the text of the opera.

When we were shown the coat and the skull, I couldn't quite believe what we were seeing. Although I was familiar with the Italian custom of exhibiting relics of saints, I had never seen anything like that.

Naturally we wanted to photograph the coat and the skull, and got permission to do so. Herbert took some pictures through the glass, but in order to have enough light to photograph he had to bring the light so close to the case that there was a reflection. When the little man who was the custodian saw that we were having trouble, he said, "Let me just take this out."

Before we realized what was happening, he had opened the case, taken out the coat, and put it on to model it for us. We made bone-chilling photographs of that man in Donizetti's death coat.

And then he said, "You will, of course, want to take pictures of the skull too." He opened the case, took Donizetti's skull out, and handed it to Herbert Senn, whose nervous fingers couldn't hold on to it. He dropped it. And I caught it! That was one of the scariest moments of my life.

We left the museum as soon as we could and went to lunch where rice with fresh white truffles took our minds off what had happened. The truffles were so good I bought some to take along to eat later. We put them in the trunk of the car. By the time we got to the hotel the smell was so horrible as to be unendurable. It was so bad I can taste it still. I have never looked at a white truffle with any interest since; just thinking of truffles brings on visions of Donizetti's desecrated grave and his skull, and our bizarre experience in his house.

In further preparation for staging *Lucia di Lammermoor,* we made a trip to Scotland to see the house of Sir Walter Scott. The bleakness of the weather and the time of the year—the sun didn't rise until ten or eleven in the morning and began setting at two or three in the afternoon—was affecting. It seemed right.

We stopped often to make photographs of the desolate countryside during the drive out from the town to the house. Some kind of dry vegetation tumbled about. The last gate on the road leading to the house was scruffy and swinging on its hinges because of the wind blowing off the moors.

As we approached the house, it looked empty. There were no visible lights. We walked all around it, looking for a sign that someone was there. When we tried the weather-beaten door, a light came on. There was a weird squeaking and scraping as it opened. A disheveled, wild-eyed caretaker let us in.

The interior was like a tomb. We felt that any minute we would hear Walter Scott screaming with a wild and terrible headache and outside neighbors would be creeping up outside the house as we had done, to listen to him and the dog howl.

Presumably the fascination with Scott's *Lucia* for Donizetti had been her madness and its manifestation. Preoccupation with madness, and the look of the Scottish moor at the time of our visit, combined to set up our concept of the opera, and determined how we would produce it and try to create a comparable atmosphere.

Our impressions and feelings remained as we read writings about madness to the carefully selected cast whom we had assembled for the production. We made sure that they knew not just of our adventures but, more important, the writings of Walter Scott and of Donizetti in this incredible opera. The quality of the writing began to work on everyone. I believe that the success of the production grew out of this attention. The music is sensitive to all psychological nuances of the drama of the script.

We had a wonderful cast. In addition to soprano Beverly Sills, as Lucia, Donald Gramm sang the bass role of the minister. We also had a superb tenor. Jaroslav Kachel, who sang the part of Ravenswood, was Czech. He was one of the most brilliant singing actors I have ever known.

He came to Boston and we had about a month's rehearsal period before the January 1969 opening (which, for America, is a lot of time). Kachel worked intensely on his part, and rehearsed with such great concern that he lifted up the performance of everybody else. He was a very fine actor, a very fine craftsman, who built his character as it related to the music. His presence inspired everyone else. In the way her characterization grew and the way her voice performed, Beverly Sills was unbelievably marvelous.

When I telephoned her to ask if she would like to sing the part, she agreed at once. Ten minutes later she called me and said, "I can't do it. I forgot. I am pregnant!" I asked her, "Were you pregnant ten minutes ago?" "Of course," she answered. Then I said, "It won't make a bit of difference. We'll adjust your costumes." That's what we did.

Herbert Senn and Helen Pond designed the set on a raised stage that came out over the orchestra pit. As some of it surrounded the pit, it was possible for the cast to come out quite far. The set was designed to look decayed. We had at that time a lady manager, a very nice lady, a very ladylike lady, whose name was Ruth McCay. She came into the theater and saw these jagged strange things coming out of the orchestra pit, and she said,

"Sarah, they didn't cut it off right. My dear, you really can't use them like that!" But of course we did and she was very upset because it did not look the way a set should look. "Couldn't we at least close the holes?" she pleaded.

With the orchestra seated in the pit, the use of special fabrics and special metal construction meant that the sound came through just fine. There were branches and roots of trees that grew out, and in between these there were the openings that the cast learned to walk carefully around.

Although it is customary for parts of *Lucia di Lammermoor,* to be cut, we did the complete opera. The production was very well received. It was in fact a great success, in my opinion, one of the best things we have ever done. Visually it was splendid. When Walter Felsenstein came to Boston several years later the model that really caught his eye was the outdoor scene in black and silver.

Our production of Mozart's *Marriage of Figaro,* also at the Shubert, was another opera very much influenced by my research into the period in which it was originally produced.

The Marriage of Figaro was a dangerous play. The playwright, Beaumarchais, was thrown into jail two or three days after the premiere. Just a few weeks after that Mozart began trying to get the rights to write an opera based on it.

I decided that the concept of peasants and overseers was not really familiar to our audience, so we made all the peasants black. This was one of my attempts to explain to the audiences what the piece was about; so often we saw, and still *do* see, Mozart's operas in really pretty costumes with shepherds and shepherdesses.

We had a wonderful, wonderful Figaro. His name was Simon Estes. He has since become a very famous singer. We have behaved in our company throughout the years in a slightly hypocritical way by saying that color doesn't matter because we won't let it matter. But it certainly intrudes visually; there's no question about that.

In our production, Susanna and all the servants were black and the Countess and the Count and Cherubino were white. I made a great effort to cast this well and I was pleased with the result. While I was in Germany I heard about this beautiful Aida who was also expected to sing the part of the Countess in *Marriage of Figaro*. I went to see *Aida*, presented by one of Felsenstein's associates in a venue outside of Berlin. Aida was ravishing. I had to return a car so I was not able to go backstage and talk to her, but I hired her anyway.

She arrived three days later than the rest of the cast. Imagine my surprise when she turned out not to be not white but kind of cream-colored. She was African American.

She came to me after the first rehearsal and said, "I have figured out the concept of this production and I think it is wonderful, but it is quite clear that you did not know that I am black." I said, "You are absolutely right," and she said, "I am perfectly happy to withdraw." I said, "I'll tell you something. I didn't know you were black and nobody else knows you are black. You are very pale. Let's make you up white and let's not tell anybody. After all, this is the theater."

When she agreed, I continued, "There's nothing false about this. The feeling will still be there and everybody will think you are white." So we did it.

After the dress rehearsal the blacks who were in the cast came up on the stage and held a prayer meeting. One of the men who sang was a black minister. He prayed and they all sang spirituals. No one asked permission. They just did it.

Only the blacks participated. All of the white singers and I remained backstage. It was chilling to experience, the "They" and "We" feeling. For the first time in my life I felt what it was like to be outside a race. I was hurt that we hadn't all been asked to participate. Today I would probably have gone out and joined them, but not then.

Rudolph Heinrich had designed a set that surrounded the stage. Thick parapet walls were placed diagonally from downstage to upstage on both sides and on the back wall. The first appearance of the peasants comes when Figaro leads a group of them to find the Count. They arrive up and over the set. The audience saw these people approaching and it was threatening.

The opera had a profound effect when we did it. It made people think twice about *Figaro*, which was what we were trying to do, without distorting it in any way.

It gave us a sense of reality of the peasant versus the nobleman. We didn't do it differently to be clever or to be politically correct or incorrect. We did it to try to give our audience the feeling of the separation of the peasants, of the dissatisfaction of the peasants with the aristocracy, and of the sense that there are feelings like that in our world today. It worked.

When it became obvious that we could not afford to remain at the unionized Shubert Theater with its limited seating, we began to search for another place to perform. We determined not to let the lack of a permanent theater deter us from producing first-class opera with the best singers we could persuade to come to Boston.

While considering venues that might prove hospitable, we found some unlikely places. We were by necessity creative in selecting and adapting our productions to spaces that were available to us. That forced us to do some of the most innovative staging of our experience. There were both advantages and drawbacks to what we came to call our Wandering Years and we tried to learn from both.

Chapter 6

The Wandering Years

Wagner's *Flying Dutchman* was an appropriate opera to present while we were ourselves so much at sea. More important, two great Wagnerian singers, Thomas Stewart and Giorgio Tozzi, were available to join our cast. Because they were singing the same roles at the Metropolitan Opera, they were in constant motion traveling between New York and Boston.

Although we had no home, we continued to perform three to five operas each season. We couldn't wait until one presentation was over to find a venue for the next; we looked at a variety of places and determined when each might be available for our use, in order to make a tentative schedule. Our venues became so out of the way, we planned to start our performances half an hour late to give the audience time to find us and then to park.

In deciding what operas we would perform, we considered many things. These included whether we thought we could sell tickets easily, whether the opera would be interesting to the general public as well as to our regular supporters, whether the opera under consideration had been performed recently, as well as what extra costs might be entailed.

We were careful to vary the selection. In the season that we did *The Flying Dutchman*, for example, we did not consider doing another nineteenth-century German opera.

We would take the set designers to the places we had located and discuss the possibilities the venues offered. We collaborated with the designers; they listened to us and we listened to them.

We concentrated on the advantages and the peculiar problems each space would offer. At the same time we were talking to managers and agents to determine which singers would be free during the three weeks or so required for rehearsals and productions, and auditioning them.

We found out about availability of singers in various ways. Sometimes I knew them personally and they would tell me when they would have time to perform with us. Sometimes I would call friends who knew when singers they knew would be free. Sometimes an agent would let us know that a certain singer was free at a specific time. Or the agent might say, we have this fantastic tenor available because a production had been canceled somewhere, and I would audition that singer.

I always kept in mind the fact that no two operas are the same. You have to have a concept for each because the problems of each production are so different. You have to have a director who makes artistic and practical decisions. That person has to be aware that sometimes in certain operas a soprano is important, sometimes a tenor is important, and sometimes the oboe is important. It depends on the opera. Creativity does not come from the opera. It comes from the way it is performed.

We staged *The Flying Dutchman* in the Kresge Auditorium of the Massachusetts Institute of Technology. The Eero Saarinen–designed auditorium was round and imparted a contemporary feeling. At one side there was a stage and room for a large orchestra. Because attached scenery could not be used in the building, Herbert Senn and Helen Pond designed an imaginative set making use of decorated platforms and beautiful screens.

The role of Senta, the daughter of a Norwegian sea captain who falls in love with the Flying Dutchman (whose fate it was to come ashore only every seven years), was sung by my friend of many years, Phyllis Curtin. The part of the Dutchman, whose curse could be lifted only by the love of a chaste woman, was sung by Thomas Stewart, the famous American baritone who performed the role at Bayreuth, alternating with the equally famous Giorgio Tozzi.

On one side of the Dutchman's ship there was a very high area that went up the side wall. The steering wheel of the Dutchman was there. From that angle the ship was projected out into the auditorium. The sailors on the ship, having crept down the aisles in the dark, sang lying on the floor, giving the audience the feeling that they were onboard ship.

There's one enormous duet with the Dutchman and Senta that Wagner did in graduated tempo changes, up and down. When Stewart came, he said to me, "I want to tell you this because we don't want to embarrass Phyllis. No soprano could sing this the way it is written. To cover I'll suddenly sing a lot faster." I told him, "I don't want you to speed up when you get there because Phyllis Curtin can sing the whole thing exactly the way it is written, beautifully." And she did. I had absolute confidence in her ability because we had studied together at the New England Conservatory. She sang with the Met, with the New York City Opera, with us, and at well-known opera houses around the world.

We used another device that created an exciting effect visually. It was a picture of the Dutchman that was projected in such a way that it grew imperceptibly each time Senta looked at it. The face got larger and larger and larger as the Dutchman grew in stature in her eyes.

Universities were hospitable to us during our search for places to perform. Sometimes the location itself suggested which opera we would stage. The Cousens Gymnasium at Tufts University became the location for *Daughter of the Regiment* by Donizetti.

The Tufts Arena is a round building that contains a track on the inside perimeter. On one wall there is a very elaborate set of stairs that goes up in geometric patterns quite high to a door. There we built our platform.

A friend who was head of the acoustical department at the Massachusetts Institute of Technology, Bob Newman, took his advanced acoustical class and followed us to various venues to tell us what to do to make the acoustics work. He suggested that Herbert Senn and Helen Pond, our stage designers, construct over the stage a set of clouds, panels that could be tilted to create a ceiling so the sound would go out to the audience rather than up.

It was a typical gymnasium with bleachers around the sides. Down the center we laid a double carpet that made a big sweep all the way across, plenty wide enough for a cart with a little donkey to drive down. On either side, chairs faced the stage.

Beverly Sills, as Marie, the Daughter of the Regiment, and Donald Gramm, as Sulpice, her guardian, were brilliant. The two of them together did some of the finest work that has ever been done for us.

During the dress rehearsal a track meet was taking place. That meant that while the orchestra was playing, there were thundering footsteps. Beverly, for a joke, had business cards printed declaring that she was Beverly Sills, Star of Stage, Screen, and Track.

At the end when Marie, the Daughter of the Regiment with her husband-to-be, Tonio, rode out in a donkey cart, the soldiers and the people sitting at the side held up pieces of cardboard that became a French flag that reached the length of the stadium.

Each venue inspired us to present opera in a more innovative way. Our motto soon became "Freedom is the opportunity to take advantage of the unexpected."

The Cage at MIT, an indoor athletic facility with a dirt floor, was a most unlikely place to perform an opera. But there we did *The Good Soldier Schweik.* A light opera with serious overtones, it was written by Robert Kurka, a gifted American composer of Czech background. It requires a wind ensemble of twenty-five instruments. Unfortunately, Robert Kurka died at thirty-five, and never saw it performed.

Based on the novel by Czech writer Jaroslav Hašek, it chronicled the adventures of a private during World War I who took all orders literally and acted on them in such a way to cause bewilderment, amusement, and consternation on the part of just about everybody.

The singers, the orchestra, and the band in our performance were dressed in military uniforms of the period of the First World War, and golf carts were costumed as army vehicles. Several of these vehicles drove the band to areas where action was taking place. The costumes, designed by Herbert Senn and Helen Pond, were squared off to look like the famous cartoons by Josef Lada that illustrated the book.

In the center of the Cage a platform sixteen feet wide and thirty feet long was built. It was about three and a half feet high with ramps at both ends that enabled people to go up and down from the stage. The stage was divided into three sections, each of which had a picture screen in the center. The screens bisected the stage so that there would be eight feet on either side. Those screens could be raised and lowered so that, with closed television, while actors were performing, their movement would be projected simultaneously on the screens.

The audience was divided into six segments with space left between the sections for the actors to move and for the cars to drive around. Making further use of the areas around which people sat, as the production was set in wartime, there was a graveyard in one place where a burial scene took place, and in another, a battle scene where trenches had been dug into the earth. Barbed wire and sandbags and cannon surrounded the battleground.

Closed-circuit television cameras traveled on golf carts masquerading as army vehicles, photographing the action and projecting it onto the screens so everybody could follow the action at all times.

In one scene, while Schweik sat on an operating table naked, above his head round screens projected the faces of three psychiatrists.

Wherever one sat there was a series of different kinds of impressions. There might be live actors facing you acting as if you were their only audience—but behind them a screen would be pulled down and the people on the other side would be getting a shadow play of the action. The performance was structured and planned so that everybody had all the various experiences at one time or another, live performance, shadow play, closed-circuit television, or special films.

This creative use of television was devised under the direction of Richard Leacock, a famous film maker who was in the MIT film department. We used other devices, including special films made with some of the singers and also movie clips from World War I, to fit certain segments of the music.

Sound was one of the most difficult problems to overcome. The band would travel in their little cars to wherever the live action was and the music would be gently amplified all over the place.

Sound was not a problem for us in our next production because it was in a theater with good acoustics. The Savoy had once been an ornate vaudeville house, but it had certainly seen better days.

The Junior League of Boston, to commemorate their sixtieth anniversary in May 1970, commissioned *The Fisherman and His Wife,* an opera composed by Gunther Schuller, to be dedicated to the children of Boston. I had raised money to finance the production and had contacted the Junior League to see if they would like to contribute to the cost and sponsor it. They spoke to Schuller directly and he agreed to do it. At a press conference I learned that he had signed a contract and that he had chosen John Updike to be his librettist.

To Schuller, *The Fisherman and His Wife* was very important. Even though it was sponsored by the Junior League, it was not an occasional piece. It was his introduction to Boston.

Helen Pond and Herbert Senn designed the sets and costumes for the opera, which was based on a Russian fairy tale. I staged and directed the performance.

I find it fascinating to work with live composers. Some you can work with easily and some don't give you any help at all. You don't work easily with Gunther Schuller. Conversations with him were not enlightening. If I didn't do precisely what he had in mind, he looked at me as if I were retarded. He managed to antagonize almost everybody involved in this production.

We performed *Louise* by Gustave Charpentier at the Flower Market, an immense round building on Tremont Street. It had originally been a cyclorama with a dome almost as wide as that of the Capitol building in Washington. It had been built to commemorate the Civil War. The building remained a museum until the cyclorama was moved to Gettysburg. The building then became a flower market.

The research we did about Charpentier in preparation for staging *Louise*, illustrates what I try to do to find out what was going on in the composer's mind. When I am working on an opera, I operate on the theory that the composer had imagined everything and that it is my job to discover as precisely as possible what his vision was.

There was a lot of material to consider for *Louise* because Charpentier wrote a detailed stage guide. He had thought through everything. He had written character sketches for each individual character, imagining their lives before the opera takes place and even afterward.

Charpentier continued to work on *Louise* even after it had been produced as an opera. He wrote a beautiful and exciting movie script and began to massage it into a form that he thought would be appropriate for the cinema. He signed a contract with a Hollywood movie company to make a film, but didn't read the fine print carefully. He discovered he would not be admitted into the rehearsal area. They didn't use his script. They didn't use his extra music. They didn't know it existed and they didn't want to know. He was heartbroken.

The opera opens with Louise and her mother having their noon meal, eating soup. Charpentier had written the exact moment when the plates should be hit by spoons. Every plate was to have a little sponge because sometimes he wanted the audience to hear that clink and sometimes he didn't. My wish is that more composers had left detailed instructions like that.

At the same time we were rehearsing on a sixty-foot-wide set that we had installed between iron pillars, the building was being converted into the Boston Center for the Arts. A week before our opening was scheduled, we were told that we would not be allowed to use the building because all the necessary codes would not be met by then. That meant that we had to postpone the opening and change some members of the cast because of their commitments elsewhere.

We extended the drama of opening night—February 24, 1971—to the outside by using sweeping spotlights and mounted police to make people who didn't often venture into that part of town (particularly at night) feel safe. One critic observed that it was "lovely to see all the society page sitting in long gowns and furs gathered in a warehouse in South Boston." Another commented that "1,700 partisans sat for four acts on the hardest seats this side of Harvard stadium and responded as though they were cushioned in luxury." The review began: "The Opera Company of Boston, the indomitable ones, transformed a South End building into a reasonably grand opera house and they presented grandly an opera that is not often seen nor heard and surely never before been presented in such surroundings."

Helen Pond and Herbert Senn, inspired by old photographs of Paris of 1900, which we found during a research trip there, designed a set to re-create a section of Montmartre. It provided an incredible backdrop of a white-and-gray city studded with tiny lights that went on and off at random.

They provided a claustrophobic little apartment where Louise lived with her family, and a big open space that was Julien's poetic lodging. Both were located in a realistic rendition of a neighborhood in Montmartre. The critics were lavish in their praise of the sets.

At the heart of the opera is the idea that the lure of the city of Paris was too much for Louise, a young girl who was susceptible to poets and the glamour of city life. Both her father and her mother were hard working people who desperately tried to fight their daughter's attraction to the city.

The part of the Noctambulist, who represented the spirit of the city at night, was performed by Tommy Rawl. He was a very fine tenor who had also been a leading dancer in the Ballet Theater. He danced the whole evening *en pointe.* Dancing on one's toes is difficult.

For the moment in the scene when the lure of the city is personified, we hired special people whose profession it was to climb high walls, to go up and put lights at the top of the dome and to install a mirror ball there. When the Noctambulist began to dance we put light on the faceted mirrors of the ball which, when turning, cast little dots of light that went all over the building. It worked perfectly and was a gorgeous piece, quite unusual before nightclubs began to use the concept.

Louise is an opera about many things, turn-of-the-century Paris, bohemian life, the generation gap, art, proletarians, and love. It opens with a clandestine duet by Julien and Louise, who meet on adjoining balconies. He is a poet and consequently considered suspect by her parents. She is a dressmaker. Their idyll is interrupted by her mother, who lets out some terrific howls of dismay when she sees Julien and then scoffs at Louise with a very funny imitation of their passionate singing. It's particularly amusing because you can understand it even if you don't know French.

Louise's father comes home and there follows a charmingly staged dinner scene where they mix their wine with water and serve each other little French things, and the father shovels in his soup like a peasant. Then with his warmest, most fatherly voice he announces, "I am happy" contentedly.

Then he opens a letter from Julien while his wife "tra la's" ominously, from behind the ironing board, suspecting it's a proposal.

The following act takes place in the street at sunrise when all the street freaks of the day come out to sing. There are bird cages and vegetable wagons and garbage barrels. There are junk dealers and ragpickers and coal gatherers and newspaper folders and a couple of cops. The effect of our presentation was enhanced by costumes that the Comédie-Française in Paris let us use.

The Noctambulist, the song-and-dance juggler who represents the pleasure of Paris, rips open his coat to reveal the scarlet lining of his coat covered in little electric lights like Montmartre. All this enthralls the bohemian set that goes around slumming and rhapsodizing.

As the sun comes up in purple and green, the scene moves to Louise's dressmaking shop. She suddenly leaves to go live with Julien, whom she finds lounging artistically before the vista of Montmartre. The two have another rapturous duet after which he sits down to mend his jacket.

There's lots of activity, and finally Louise is flooded with flowers. Lights go swirling around the cyclorama. The dancers are surrounded by a circle of urchins and then sail away, and that's a romanticized view of life in the slums of Paris around 1900.

Louise's mother, played convincingly by Eunice Albert, comes to retrieve her daughter, telling her father is dying from missing her. Louise returns home but it looks pretty pale after what she has been through.

At home, she gazes out of the window, sighing, "Paris . . . Paris," until her father shouts, "Enough! Go away! Go!!!" Then he throws her out of the house and glares out at the city, "Ah! Paris," and that's it. Nobody dies.

Critic Elliot Norton liked every aspect of the production, including the sets, the music (which he described as "although not one of the masterworks of all time, wonderfully melodious"), and the cast. He chose for exceptional praise the portrayal of Donald Gramm as the overworked father whose only happiness was his daughter. He described his characterization as masterful, with every nuance of voice and gesture right—particularly the last scene in which he slowly, disbelievingly, comes to see Louise as a mature, sensual, and independent woman.

We had reached, finally, the end of our Wandering Years.

Chapter 7

The Orpheum Theater

The Orpheum Theater, for a time called the Aquarius, was a strange place. Built as a vaudeville theater, it had a small stage, no backstage area at all, and a pit that meant that the audience was very much aware of the presence of the orchestra. That was a good thing, I think. It was nice.

After arrangements had been made to use the theater, our president, Dr. Laszlo Bonis, who was noted for having devised the system for astronauts to practice weightlessness, announced to the board of trustees, "Now you can have a permanent seat for your subscription." The retort of one of the trustees was, "Yes, and we can take it home and repair it."

We rented space at a beauty school next door because there were only three tiny dressing rooms, and I used one of them. Once I was sitting in my dressing room talking with Beverly Sills when a rat came in and walked right past us. It didn't bother us a bit because we were used to seeing rats. One of the problems Boston has had and still has is that much of the city sits on reclaimed land. One thing that helped was that there was nothing we could do about it. It wasn't that the place was dirty or that we had been leaving things for the rats to eat. Every building in that area was infested that way. The city continues to struggle to do something about it.

Despite the difficulties presented by the theater we managed to have some wonderful productions. One was *Don Carlos*. With the help of much-appreciated financial support from Meg and Robert

Tobin, and access to the materials arranged by my British friend, Andrew Porter, we were able to do the research necessary to present the original version in French for the first time in the United States. We retrieved two long and beautiful music interludes that had been cut out of the original performance and pasted over because the opera was considered to be too long.

We also gave the first American performance of Prokofiev's *War and Peace* at the Orpheum. That production led to my first appearance at Carnegie Hall and guest- appearances in several cities.

We used the extraordinary imaginative and technical skills of Herbert Senn and Helen Pond for most of our stage sets. Constructed in a former brick factory in South Boston where they oversaw the production of the sets, a green Trojan horse twenty-two feet high was their most grandiose accomplishment. *The Trojans,* by Hector Berlioz, a massive mid-nineteenth-century opera, is two operas actually. Based on Virgil's *Aeneid,* it recounts events of the Trojan Wars and the love story of Dido and Aeneas.

As it had never been produced in its entirety in America, reviewers from across the country came to see it. Having battled sleet and snow in early February 1972, to get to the theater, they were enthusiastic about our production. We presented *The Fall of Troy* and *The Trojans in Carthage* on subsequent nights and in a Sunday matinee and evening performance. Our performers included Grace Bumbry, Giorgio Tozzi, and Régine Crespin.

Troy fell because the Greeks brought a great wooden horse into the city and retreated, leaving it there. In our production, the gates of Troy opened and an enormous horse came in and slowly crossed the stage. Everybody gasped when it slipped under the proscenium with a tolerance of less than an inch and rolled off the stage onto a platform where it stood for a very long time. A reviewer from Houston commented that even in Texas horses don't come that big.

There were other monumental props. One was Neptune on a pedestal with his trident towering above the stage. Another was

Pallas Athena in her temple high up in the front of the theater, wearing a helmet and holding a huge shield and spear. The city walls appeared thick enough and strong enough to withstand anything.

Boxes at the front of the theater contained platforms accessed by stairs, enabling movement during the opera to be vertical as well as horizontal. One reviewer remarked that Cassandra, running about trying vainly to warn the Trojans of the perfidy of the Greeks, went up and down stairs almost continually, making it a wonder that she had any breath to sing.

The audience came back from intermission and saw that the horse was still there. After intermission it was night. Suddenly the stomach of the horse opened up, rope ladders came down and many, many soldiers climbed down from inside that horse. We gave the impression that still others came out, and there was a big battle onstage.

We had put children dressed as soldiers in the horse and also used little kids to parade up and down on the ramparts of the city, which were quite tall. They looked so far away, indicating a perspective that could not exist on the narrow stage that, as the cast performed on the stage, they seemed to be normal soldiers in the distance.

With the tumultuous music of Berlioz underlying the effect, the destruction of Troy was impressive. As flames that appeared to be caused by flares lobbed over the thick walls reached toward the ceiling, the walls collapsed with plenty of simulated dust and smoke. When Neptune fell from his pedestal he landed very close to where I was conducting, giving the audience another jolt. The appearance of Hector's ghost, projected over the scene of destruction, added drama to the mayhem.

The Trojans as described by one Boston critic, "was more a spectacle than an opera, more exciting visually than musically." But, he added, "the visual crescendo tended to, but could not quite obscure the fact that there were some fine voices being heard."

Harry Neville, a critic from Houston, commented that the monumental work came off spectacularly on the narrow, basically inadequate stage of a movie house long past its prime. He noted "magnificent sets, good singing, respectable orchestra, fine acting and conducting, excellent stage movement" as some of the factors that made the production "an always engaging, sometimes brilliantly successful event." He added that the Opera Company of Boston could claim a "proud moment in American operatic history."

One of the productions we did was *Don Quichotte,* a turn-of-the-century French opera by Jules Massenet. My mother very much wanted us to do it. She had seen it in Chicago several times. Oh, she loved it. Herbert and Helen had a lot of fun with my mother while designing the sets. We considered it her production.

I did research in preparation for both directing and conducting the opera. I went to Paris where I found the original manuscript at the Paris Opera together with a great deal of material concerning it.

This is what I discovered: There was in Paris at the time the opera was written an enormously tall, thin, emaciated poet named Henri Cain who had serious mental problems. From time to time he was in mental institutions, where he had delusions that he himself was Don Quichotte. The poet understood that when he was ill he thought he was Don Quichotte.

He wrote a play that was a brilliant study of what is real and what is imaginary. It asked such questions as, Is reality what you see on the stage? Is reality in life what you dream, believe, or imagine? How do you ground your life? The play was based indirectly on the Don Quixote–Sancho Panza novel by Cervantes. Massenet was so impressed by Cain's play that he asked the author for permission to set it to music in an opera.

The tragedy of the poet was that he never got to see the opera. When he heard that it was being presented in Paris, he managed to escape from the institution where he was being held, walked and hitchhiked for several days. Although he developed pneumonia, he almost reached the door to the theater before he died.

I read the play before beginning a serious study of the opera. It was clear to me that his approach presented an entirely different concept from what was traditionally produced on the stage.

I had seen *Don Quichotte* in East Berlin, where they had the advantage of the work of the phenomenal puppet maker in the Berliner Ensemble, Eddie Fisher. He created an incredible horse and donkey whose movements were controlled by people inside. They were so endearing that I said if we are going to do this we must have such a horse and donkey. I went to Eddie Fisher and he agreed to make for us costumes similar to those he had made for the Komische Oper.

If I had thought it through, I would have asked him to make them look rather different, because philosophically what we were doing was not the same as had been done at the Komische Oper.

To explain what it was all about, and to make sure the audience understood, we included an explanation, including some of the text written by the poet.

The animals—the horse and the donkey—were peopled by basketball players and track people from Boston College. The puppetry was so detailed that the horse could bend down and his tongue would come out. He could flick flies off himself. He could drink water. He could twitch one ear. He could twitch both ears. The students wanted to come and rehearse and rehearse. They loved what they were doing. They got so good that the animals had distinctive personalities. They weren't two guys inside, they were animals.

There was one terrible moment when Don Quichotte leapt up on the back of the horse. He was supposed to get up gradually so he wouldn't hurt the people inside, but he forgot that Rossinante was not real.

There was a theater inside a theater in the first act. It was designed so that its proscenium was identical to the proscenium at the Orpheum, which had Tiffany glass all around backlit with lights. There was one wonderful moment when the lights of our

theater lit up and the lights of the theater that was moving around
lit up at the same time. The effect was incredible.

Because my mother's strongest memory was of Fyodor Chalia-
pin, the creator of the title role, going around and around the
windmill, Herbert and Helen designed a fantastic windmill. We
found a big, tall Don Quichotte whose major qualification was
his height. We also had a double for our Don Quichotte. He was
furnished by a British company that specialized in making people
fly. What happened was, he would strike at the windmill, and finally, as he stood as high as he could, the sword got caught, it
seemed, in the windmill. Then the flying really started. This man
flew all the way up and went around and around and around. I
have never seen any greater theatrical sensation. People screamed
because of the unexpectedness of it. They believed for a moment
that it was real. It was a big coup de théâtre.

Donald Gramm, who sang the part of Sancho Panza, said to
me on opening night, "Sarah, you're wonderful, but there is one
thing you do badly. That's curtain calls. Please let me take care of
it tonight." I said, "Donald, you're on."

He let the animals take the curtain calls. There was a split in
the center of the curtain and a horse's face peeked out and looked
around, then came out. The audience went wild. Then the donkey
came out. Donald had taught them to bow. It was great.

One thing still irritates me enormously. The *New York Times* reviewer, having seen the opera at the Komische Oper, where the
only thing that was similar was the horse and the donkey, wrote
that we had copied the entire production. He had a copy of our
program and if he had read it, it would have been obvious to him
that our production was based on a totally different concept.

Helen Pond and Herbert Senn, by the time they designed the
sets and costumes for *Don Quichotte* had been our principal set—
and often, costume—designers, for several years. We worked
closely together. They invariably managed to conceptualize both
our concrete and our arcane ideas.

We presented the American premiere of Roger Sessions's opera, *Montezuma*, at the Orpheum on March 31, 1976. Our audience heard one of the great American operas performed for the first time in English. Its world premiere had been in German.

More than ten years earlier, in 1964, in West Berlin, my mother and I had attended the premiere as well as some of the rehearsals preceding it. When the people who did the production came out to take the curtain call, they were booed. There was a man sitting next to my mother who did this. She was horrified beyond anything. She turned and beat him with her fists. It was one of the funniest things I have seen and became a story that Roger Sessions liked very much to tell.

He indicated that he was not completely pleased with the score on which he had worked for many years. He felt that the libretto in German made the opera sound ponderous and that the Deutsche Oper singing was too elaborate.

Montezuma, concerning the conquest of the Aztecs in Mexico in the sixteenth century, was set to a libretto by Giuseppe Antonio Borgese. It portrays the conflict between the Mexican emperor Montezuma, and his Spanish conqueror, Hernán Cortés. It was based on journals by Bernai Díaz, a soldier who accompanied Cortés. Díaz is one of the characters in the opera, the narrator who sits and writes and sings.

In our production the role of Montezuma was sung by John Moulson and the role of Bernai Díaz was sung by Donald Gramm. John Moulson was an American tenor who sang at Bayreuth. He became a Kammersänger in Germany and was the person who introduced me to the legendary Intendant of the Komische Oper, Walter Felsenstein.

The essence of the opera is the tragic inability of the lieutenants of Cortés and of Montezuma to communicate successfully with each other. The two leaders were more sympathetic to one another's ideas.

The end result was that Montezuma was captured and stoned to death. The stoning of Montezuma happened when Cortés was away and his young firebrand chief lieutenant was in charge. This led to book burnings and all kinds of horrible things Cortés didn't want. It's a very perceptive story. Most of it is based on historical fact. It has wonderful music.

Joining me on a research trip to Mexico in preparation for our production, were our stage manager, Pat Ryan, filmmaker Richard Leacock, and board member Susan Timkin. At the Archaeological Museum in Mexico City, we met a curator who was an expert on Cortés.

He took us to the coast from which we retraced the journey of Cortés from where he landed, across the countryside, to Mexico City. Part of the way we walked; part of the way we traveled in cars; and part of the way we were mounted on burros. That part resulted in amusing films made by Richard Leacock. This journey enabled us to get a feel for the countryside.

We made contact with the Ballet Folklórico in Mexico City and that led to their making costumes for us and also in their coming to Boston and dancing in our production of *Montezuma*.

While conferring with Roger Sessions, who lived and taught at Princeton University, I was fascinated to try to determine the way he worked, the way he thought about things, and the way his music functioned. I taped many hours of conversation with him about his opera. He came to rehearsals. He loved the production and wrote beautiful things about it.

After making do at the Orpheum Theater for several years, eight years after the Opera Company of Boston was formed, and twelve years after the Opera Group gave that first performance in the Boston Public Garden, an incredible opportunity presented itself to us. Members of the family of one of our board members, who chose to remain anonymous, offered to make it possible for us to buy the Keith Memorial Theater on Washington Street. At last we would have a permanent home.

Chapter 8

The Opera House

That building became The Opera House. Built originally in 1928 as a vaudeville theater, it was impressive both inside and out, with a stunning white marble façade. Although it retained much of its original glamour and luster—including brass railings and magnificent chandeliers—located on Washington Street in a decrepit part of Boston, it was dowdy and run-down. It had been used as a movie theater called the Savoy. It was the same Savoy where I had conducted Gunther Schuller's *The Fisherman and his Wife* several seasons before.

A cinder-block wall had been constructed along the edge of the stage so two different films could be shown at the same time. One screening room was located on the stage and the other was in the auditorium. We blasted out the cinder-block wall, did basic cleaning and painting, and enlarged the orchestra pit. The most difficult part proved to be getting up the stage rigging, the rope system from which sets are hung.

From the beginning our company used union stagehands working with theater students. We hired eight stagehands. They were paid more than the union scale on the theory that they were teaching skills and crafts that were handed down from father to son, skills that the students couldn't learn at the university. The union stagehands did this relatively happily because they knew that we didn't have any money. They also knew that we would bring in students from the local universities and from the University of Wisconsin who would assist them.

To the students this was an exciting opportunity. They were in Boston for ten days or two weeks, away from their college campuses doing something professional. They wanted to work all the time. They were terribly respectful to the stagehands who taught them how to tie knots and do other useful and necessary things. They would go away and there would be no threat to the local union. We paid the students just enough to live on while they stayed in college dorms.

In Boston the Stage Hands Union at that time had slightly under a hundred members. It was father to son and they controlled all the jobs. They had a system in which every Friday night the jobs were assigned for the next week by the union. The first jobs went to the sons and daughters of the leaders; then if more workers were needed, they would let some of the kids of union members work.

When we acquired the theater, I went to the union to tell them we were about to do the rigging, and that we needed their help. They said they had decided that they wouldn't work in our new theater unless it was all union.

I explained that we had been given a building but we didn't have any money. "Aw, they can give you the money," they insisted. I said, "Not possible," and they said, "Then we're sorry. Just go out and do it with students. Forget us."

I talked with three technical directors whom I knew, including one who had taught in Boston who was then working in New York. They all came with groups of students and did indeed do all the rigging—and perfectly.

Nine days after we acquired the theater we presented our first opera. It was *Tosca.*

The union of stagehands picketed us. Fortunately, we had a good labor lawyer on our board, so in about two hours the pickets were removed.

Union members were not allowed to take jobs that people already had. This applied to all unions, including the box office union and the company managers' union, as well as unions representing people who cleaned the rest rooms and the ushers. Our staff did all these things so union members couldn't come in.

On opening night I went out to speak to the audience to explain that all the amenities, including the ladies' and gentlemen's rooms weren't ready yet, but they would be soon. A microphone for me was taken out onto the stage, and, life being what it was, the microphone didn't work. I had to speak to people all over the auditorium, including way up at the top. I didn't have any trouble being understood by everyone because the people who built theaters for stand-up comedians before microphone days knew how to incorporate excellent acoustics.

Magda Olivero was a distinguished Italian singer who came out of retirement to sing in *Tosca.* Other distinguished members of the cast were Giorgio Tozzi and Robert Trehy. I staged the production and William Fred Scott conducted. We used the sets that Rudolf Heinrich had designed for us.

When he was designing that first production for us, Heinrich and I met in Rome because we wanted to get the sense of history, what really happened at the time the opera transpires. We went to the original sites. We went to the church where it had originally been set and then to the church where it had been moved. We photographed and photographed and photographed in detail all the places that were settings for the opera.

We went to the Farnese Palace which had become the French Embassy, photographed it, and continued to the Castel Sant'Angelo. The last act plays at the top of the Castel Sant'Angelo, which at the beginning of the nineteenth century, when the opera was set, was being used as a prison.

With the help of *Time* magazine, it was arranged for us to go up to the top of the Castel Sant'Angelo. We paid the caretaker to stay up all night with us there. One of the things I wanted to do was to record some sounds. Puccini wrote music in which he imagined what one would have heard from the top of Castel

Sant'Angelo. He included bells and a shepherd singing and other night sounds in his music.

To get there we had to go up planks suspended by ropes. There was a very shaky rope along the side. I didn't dare look down. I felt as if I were at the top of a circus tent, but higher.

Because I had made such a fuss about going there, *Time* magazine had sent a photographer. Also, the Voice of America had sent someone who would record every word and every sound, so I couldn't chicken out.

I had to be brave and I had to look nonchalant. I thought, "I can't do it, but I have to do it," and I did it. Going up was terrifying but once there, I told myself, "The only solution for this is, I will not come down. They can send a helicopter for me. I will break an ankle or do whatever is necessary, to make this possible."

Because there are so many church bells in Rome, certain bells are rung only on certain days and ours was not one of them. What we heard were trucks, and a million little tiny birds flying around that made so much noise you could hardly hear yourself think. Nevertheless, we waited for hours to see what was going to happen.

After a time on top of the Castel Sant'Angelo, Rudolph Heinrich, who was a kind of prankster, found out that the execution bell, which was one of the things we wanted to record to use in the show had not been used for many many years. It was broken. The warden pointed to it hanging out from the building.

All of a sudden Heinrich shimmied up a wall and got himself inside the bell and kind of swung out over Rome as he was fixing it so it could ring. All we could see was the bell and Rudolph's legs.

After such bravado I could not insist on being removed by helicopter. After devouring the meager breakfast somebody had brought, we started down the rope ladder. In such a situation you don't want to look down, but you've got to look down enough to see where your foot goes next. When we got to the side of the castle it was worse, because where stone steps had been cut out of the wall there was nothing to hold on to.

I had said we wanted to hear the sound of the turn of a key opening a creaking prison door. Well, *that* was something that the warden could arrange. He had us stop at each of the dank cells and listen to the key screech in the rusty locks. We recorded at least a dozen of these unpleasant sounds before we finally reached bottom.

We had wondered why Puccini changed the church. Puccini wrote a great Te Deum at the close of the first act, which takes place in the Attavanti Chapel. When the Cardinal comes in there is this enormous sound. I asked if we could record this Te Deum. We were informed that nobody except a certain elderly priest was allowed to play the organ, and he had terrible cataracts. He couldn't see the music, except very vaguely, we were told, but he could play the organ. It was arranged for him to come and play for us.

While we were waiting for the organist there was a choir rehearsal of little choir boys. They were singing in English so badly off-pitch it was just incredible. A similar rehearsal takes place in the first scene of the opera, so we captured that on tape.

When the ancient priest who could hardly see played the organ, I realized why Puccini had moved the location: because without any question it was the loudest organ I have ever heard in my life. For the Te Deum Puccini must to have said to himself, "That's the organ I want!"

All of this I described to the singers in our original production, and in subsequent productions as well. The cast heard the tapes and saw the photographs, and this helped them share the sense of reality we had felt while we were in Rome.

Rudolph Heinrich, who had gone all over Rome, sometimes photographing with distortion lenses, made a collage of impressions and used them to create a beautiful set.

The most expensive opera we produced in the Opera House was *Medea* by Luigi Cherubini, a native of Italy who wrote in French.

In *Medea* the music was written with French dialogue. A good portion of the evening is spent reciting text in the style of a Greek play. Because it was directed by Greeks, I believed there had also been traditional musical instruments accompanying the long recitations in between the arias and the dances.

I engaged a talented young Greek composer who had done a lot of writing for Greek plays and who had also studied the styles of performances in ancient Greece.

For us he wrote music for Greek ethnic instruments, four or five of them, to be played under the spoken text. He brought musicians from Greece to play these instruments. The spoken text was in Greek, and the part of the text that was sung was in French.

The Greek costume designer whom we hired dressed the French people as they would have been dressed in France and the Greek actors as they would have been dressed at a play at that historical time. They wore big, tall shoes, and their costumes were all white, so there was no question of who were the Greeks.

We used Greek actors entirely. Intoning in Greek, they stole the show. I thought it worked superbly. One problem that I could have corrected, and I would correct if I did it again, was that the Greek music and the Greek dialogue were louder than the French music and the singing in French. Even though the Greek tradition is of declaiming, the music of the French should have been, for balance, more impressive.

The sets were sculptural, mostly white. Jonathan Gardella, a young designer who accompanied me when I went to Greece to make arrangements to have the costumes made, devised a huge staircase, an enormous bridge that went across the stage, and a number of caryatids, those ladies that hold up buildings. It was very impressive. He had the assistance of an excellent set designer in Jerusalem where the sets were built.

When Bob DiDomenica telephoned and said he had written an opera and he would like to play it for me, I said, "Fine." I suggested he come and see me the next Sunday at ten o'clock in the morning. He was very excited when he arrived. He said he had driven to Lincoln (where I lived) the night before to make sure he could find my house without being late.

He played the music for me, and his wife, who was a pianist, also played it for me. I was very impressed with it. *The Balcony* is a very exciting story with an unusual musical construction.

So I said, "Let's try to do it. Our difficulty will be that it will cost a lot of money." He assured me that he had backers who would help, and they did, generously.

Because it was an unknown opera, not many tickets were sold to the initial performances. Our ticket income was so far below our expectation that we had to borrow money to cover operating costs.

We were then able to present it several times. It was shocking and shaking, but not shocking to be shocking. It is a very strong opera. We gave a good performance, well done and well put together. It had a wonderful cast, and it just worked. DiDomenico's parents, who had been consistently supportive of his musical career, were gratified.

The Balcony, in 1990, would be the last opera we would produce at the Opera House.

BEYOND BOSTON

Sarah did not want to write an autobiography. She preferred to write a memoir concerned with music. She did not hesitate, though, to mention her personal past in relation to her world of music. The result was that even though she didn't plan to write an autobiography, in the context of her extraordinary life in music, in effect she did.

First, she is a four-year-old experiencing the excitement of sleeping in a train for the first time. She was on her way to Chicago with her one-eighth–size violin to give a concert. She doesn't remember what she played. It was whatever she had heard her teacher play because she could not read music.

She went with her mother to concerts and to see theatrical performances regularly.

While her mother (whom she described as "perfect") worked as a concert performer, a music teacher, and conductor, Sarah spent summers with her great-aunt Emily, a pianist who taught her how to play the piano, and her great-uncle Ed in Maryville, Missouri. Because her parents had been divorced when she was an infant, she scarcely knew her father.

She said that Aunt Emily had a novel way to discipline her. If Sarah did something of which she disapproved, she would lie on the floor, kick her heels, and make funny noises. It embarrassed Sarah to see her do that, so she tried to be good. Her Uncle Ed liked to have little kids visit him in his insurance office. He would demonstrate to Sarah's friends how his repeater watch worked and give them nickels for ice cream cones.

We meet Sarah's adored stepfather, Professor Henry Alexander, the last of the gentlemen who courted her mother. She followed his suggestion that she enroll as a psychology student at the University of Arkansas where he taught. She had graduated from high school and was twelve years old.

Although her mother hoped she would pledge her own sorority, Sarah, who was too young to have an interest in that, would dress up as if she were on her way to the rush parties, but sneak off to see a movie instead.

We learn about a baby brother, George, who, when he was three (while his father, who was supposed to be looking after him, had a nap), climbed out of his crib, took off his clothes, collected two sticks of butter out of the refrigerator and went for a stroll in the neighborhood.

Sarah was just thirteen when she left for Boston to study at the New England Conservatory of Music. She was studying violin at Hendrickson College when her teachers there, who also taught at the Juilliard School of Music, recognized her talent and recommended that she study in Boston.

She says that her mother, trying to settle down as a faculty wife and a new mother in a small university town with little to do, became depressed after Sarah went away. It is easy to understand why Sarah, because of her own experience, loved Gustave Charpentier's *Louise* so much and produced it with such gusto.

Years later, after being widowed, her mother, Margaret, came to live with Sarah, and toward the end of her life suffered from dementia. When Margaret died, Sarah was surprised to learn from family records that her mother was several years older than she was assumed to be. Her mother's mother had done her bit to help the deception by tearing off the corners of her report cards that had dates written on them.

Sarah confided that there was a discrepancy in her own age as well. Because she wanted to smoke and to drive—two things her great-uncle Ed had taught her—and "play gigs," she pretended to be several years older than she actually was when she went to live in Boston. That is why, when she died, her obituaries didn't agree. Some suggested that she pretended to be younger than she actually was.

Eventually her brother George also became Sarah's responsibility. He experienced a mental breakdown while he was in medical school. She arranged for him to live in a special-care facility in Boston.

While Sarah and I were working on her memoir at her house in Lincoln, George sometimes came out on the train to visit. He was handsome, soft-spoken, and considerate, as well as concerned that he might miss his train back to Boston. After a time he became sick and died, leaving Sarah with no living relative.

It's understandable why she became engrossed with her production of *Lucia di Lammermoor* (in which the heroine goes mad) and in the lives of Donizetti and Sir Walter Scott, both of whom suffered from bouts of madness. She was proud of Joan Sutherland's depiction of Elvira in *I Puritani* (in which Elvira too goes mad), and of the riveting performance of Shirley Verrett as Lady Macbeth.

In her narrative, Sarah chose not to disentangle events in order to discuss them in chronological order. The chapters in "Beyond Boston" appear to be a flashback, but that's an illusion. Except for her earliest adventures at Tanglewood, and with the New England Opera Theater, her experiences with the American National Opera, in New York City, with other regional operas, and in many cities across America, were occurring simultaneously with her incomparable productions in Boston.

She spent several summers at Tanglewood, first as a student, then as a teacher. It was there that she became a lifelong friend of Leonard Bernstein. She first describes him as an adult of twenty-one or twenty-two while she was still a student.

The most important person in her musical development, and specifically in opera, was her faculty adviser and mentor, Boris Goldovsky. He was head of the opera department of the New England Conservatory as well as head of the opera department at Tanglewood during summers. His voice was familiar to Americans from his intermission commentaries during the *Metropolitan Opera on the Air* Saturday broadcasts.

As Sarah became well known in Boston for doing what Goldovsky himself had not been able to do—present world-class opera there—their relationship became strained to the point that Goldovsky would not speak to her for several years. Toward the end of his life, however, he relented and came to a party she arranged at her house to which she invited musicians with whom they both had worked. He and Sarah never met again.

Chapter 9

Tanglewood

Although Boston remained through the years the focus for my conducting and directing, I have always been receptive to the possibility of working beyond Boston. I worked simultaneously in other places at the same time we were presenting opera in Boston. Tanglewood, located conveniently two hours from Boston and two hours from New York, provided my first opportunity to do that.

In the 1940s, Tanglewood was a place of much intensity. It was a very important place then. It was a wonderful place. One had the impression that what was happening at Tanglewood in the summer was the most important thing that was happening in music—and it was. Everyone there felt as if anointed. Each concert was important. Every department, including choral music, chamber music, opera, composition, conducting. and directing, was important. The best musicians were gathered there not to do what they needed to do commercially but to perform the music they wanted to perform, to present the programs they wanted to present, and to explore what they wanted to explore.

I went to Tanglewood first as a student. I had begun my musical career when I was very young. Because my mother, a musician, had many friends in the symphony orchestra in Kansas City where we lived, we always had chamber music at home.

My mother had a friend whom I liked very much, a violinist whose name was Helen Dvorak. I began to study violin with her. First I had a one-eighth–size violin, then a one-quarter–size, and than a one-half–size. When I was four, she took me with her on the train to Chicago where I performed a concert. I played by imitation. I had learned certain pieces and played them like she did because I had not learned to read music I remember more about that train ride than I do about the concert; the ride was much more exciting.

I adored the stepfather whom my mother married when I was older. Because my parents were divorced when I was an infant, I scarcely knew my biological father, who was a chemistry professor and a farmer. I considered Henry Alexander my father. He taught me various things. He said, "There's plenty of time to do everything. You can study all the music you want to study. You can take all the violin lessons you want, but why don't you study something else, too, in the university?" I chose to study, in addition to music, the psychology of learning at the University of Arkansas, where he taught.

I also studied violin at Hendricks College, a small Methodist college in Conway, Arkansas. The music staff was sent by the Juilliard School in New York. One of those teachers suggested that I study violin at the New England Conservatory in Boston.

While I was at Hendricks College, we formed a little group of friends who did not like to get up early in the morning. If you had breakfast on campus you had to go to chapel first. We declared ourselves a breakfast club and we had breakfast every night about ten o'clock in town. We created a little dance step and as we skipped through the quiet streets of Conway we chanted, "James James Morrison Morrison Weatherby George Depree took great care of his mother even though he was only three!" from A. A. Milne's *When We Were Very Young.*

A member of our group was Eugene Haun, a very bright student who had very little money. He decided that as he could afford to attend neither the University of Arkansas nor Harvard, he might as well go to Harvard—which he did as an honor student on scholarship.

After two years in college, I reluctantly left my family, which by then included a handsome baby boy with golden curls named George Alexander, and went to Boston to study music at the New England Conservatory of Music.

I left Arkansas with my father's "secret of learning" ringing in my ears. He said that what was important was not *what* you study but *with whom* you study. He suggested that I major in professors. He said that if I found a wonderful, brilliant professor, it wouldn't make any difference what he was teaching. I should learn from him, try to determine how his mind worked, what he considered important, how he behaved, and how he reacted.

I found that wonderful teacher in Boris Goldovsky. While a student at the conservatory I was assigned Boris Goldovsky as a faculty adviser. He was head of the opera department. I studied stage direction and had conducting lessons with him and became his assistant.

I came to Boston to study violin with Richard Burgin, the concertmaster of the Boston Symphony. He was a brilliant taskmaster of whom I lived in awe and terror. His teaching method was to assemble three or four students in his apartment at the same time. We all worked on the same piece so one got a lesson while the others sat in the next room and listened.

During my first visit to that sacred place, I met Ruth Posselt, Burgin's wife, who was a wonderful concert violinist. From her I got a glimpse of the Bostonians' view of the rest of the United States. She told me she was about to undertake a concert tour way out west, in Cleveland.

Because Burgin was not head of the violin department, we students who had chosen him over the reigning guru of the violin often felt like we were an endangered species. When I was assigned Boris Goldovsky as a faculty adviser, I was glad to find him young and charming, as well as an extraordinary pianist.

I began attending his opera classes, where I made the astonishing discovery that one could spend one's life in music and in the theater simultaneously. Although these were my two great passions, I had never thought about opera as a serious art form. I soon fell under the spell of opera as Goldovsky envisioned it and this changed my life.

I went to Goldovsky and asked him what I would have to do to work in opera, considering how little I knew. He told me not to be afraid, that he had had to learn what he knew. He became my teacher, my guide, and my champion.

My parents, who had sacrificed a great deal to send me to Boston to become a violinist, were not enchanted with this new goal of mine and it would be many years before they accepted it.

The Goldovskys took me into their home as an au pair. My responsibility was to take care of their two young children early in the mornings, and get them off to school. I got room and board, a place to practice, and pocket money.

Living with the Goldovskys, I learned what it meant to live a life in music. She was a soprano and they were exploring music, making music, playing music, all day long.

I continued attending classes at the conservatory, still studying violin. I also began studying viola with a brilliant French violist of the Boston Symphony, George Fourrel. With Fourrel and his friends I was able to play chamber music often. That gave great richness to my life in those days.

It was wartime and most young male musicians were in the armed services. When there was a vacancy in the Minneapolis Symphony, then conducted by Dmitri Mitropoulos, for the assistant first chair viola, I auditioned and was offered the position. I was to have been paid the handsome salary of seventy dollars a week. My parents were delighted. It meant I might be playing solos, and going back in the direction of the musical life they envisioned for me.

At that time Boris Goldovsky was starting an opera company with virtually no money but with great enthusiasm. He was surrounded by a number of remarkably fine young singers, many of whom he had trained and imbued with his principles of artistic integrity. These included an intimate relationship between music and theater and the artist's responsibility to the work he was performing.

To counter my seventy-dollar-a-week contract I was offered an additional ten dollars a week by Goldovsky. Without the slightest hesitation I gratefully accepted his offer, and I am still glad I did.

Continuing to live with his family, I became a translator, a chorusmaster, the property master, and his general assistant. He taught me stage directing, conducting, and diplomacy. His precepts of the relationships between musical structure of an operatic scene and the arrangement of singing actors on the stage to bring out and clarify musical structure formed the basis of everything I have done since.

As I became increasingly interested in conducting, I studied both with Goldovsky and at Tanglewood. Although I was the only young woman in the class, conducting seemed a natural thing for me to do.

My mother was a concert pianist and, in addition to teaching music at school, and giving private lessons, she conducted three church choirs. She had studied music at Northwestern and at Juilliard.

During the Depression, after my grandfather's bank in Nodaway County, Missouri, failed, we moved to Kansas City, Kansas. My grandfather came to Kansas City with only a hundred dollars in his pocket. He had used his resources to pay people who had deposited money in his bank and lost it when the bank failed. He sold insurance. After my grandfather died (when I was seven), my mother supported her mother and me. She was a wonderful mother and I wanted to be like her.

At the conservatory, while I was still a student, I staged Ralph Vaughan Williams's *Riders to the Sea*. We performed it with piano. We had no scenery. The outline of the house was made with bentwood chairs. A fellow student who sang in that opera was Phyllis Curtin. The next summer Goldovsky suggested that we put it on the program at Tanglewood and that I direct it. For that performance I had the services of a scenic designer and an orchestra.

Goldovsky took me to Tanglewood as a student, and he introduced me to Serge Koussevitzky, another fabled musician with a Russian background. Koussevitzky was a great, great man. I shall never forget the first time I heard his Boston Symphony perform, the extraordinary sound it made.

He instituted the Berkshire Festival at Tanglewood. Tanglewood was his dream. When one of his admirers expressed discomfort with the idea of concerts under a tent in the woods, he announced, "Madame, the temple is where the priests are!"

Koussevitzky always wore a cape and looked handsomely turned out, particularly in the evenings when it was chilly. He deplored the dress of some of the younger students. Leonard Bernstein, an irrepressible young man in his twenties, wrote a little jazz tune along the lines of "We may look like apes but come the revolution we'll all wear capes!" There was a time when Lenny came late to a concert and conducted in tennis shoes. That created a great scandal. Koussevitzky was beside himself. He made sure that everybody understood that it was a great honor to conduct an orchestra, and that your shoes are very important.

The first summer I was a student at Tanglewood—1946—was the year that *Peter Grimes*, commissioned from Benjamin Britten by Koussevitzky, had its premiere there. It had had its world premiere the year before in London. It was an exciting time, a topsy-turvy time because the man who was to have staged the opera backed out, and at the last minute they had to get somebody else. Although it threatened to upset many of the programs at Tanglewood, it wasn't allowed to do so.

Peter Grimes, was concerned with the upheaval at a fishing village in Suffolk when two young apprentices of the fisherman, Peter Grimes, die, one after the other.

Just after World War II there were no regular scenic materials available, but a superb Czech scenic designer, Richard Richtarik, worked at Tanglewood. He made the design set mostly out of corrugated paper and bits and pieces of things, and it was one of the most beautiful stage sets I have ever seen.

Although I was technically a viola student, I was also studying stage direction, and in that guise I was able to attend most rehearsals. At the end, after Benjamin Britten himself arrived in Tanglewood, I was put backstage with a score to give light cues. Lenny Bernstein was conducting. He came backstage just before he went down into the pit to begin. He was terribly nervous and Koussevitzky was encouraging him, telling him he would do brilliantly.

I was sitting there with a music stand and a score. Bernstein looked at me and he said, "What are you doing?" and I said, "I'm giving light cues," and he said, "I hope you read music," and without thinking much I said, "I hope you do too!" That was the beginning of our friendship.

I staged a student performance of his one-act opera *Trouble in Tahiti* at Tanglewood. He was so nervous and diplomatic that he asked advice from everyone about his opera as it was being prepared. He followed all the advice he received and kept changing things. He was open to suggestions in a way I could never be. Finally I told him that *he* was in charge and should act that way. The official premiere of *Trouble in Tahiti* would be in 1952 at Brandeis University where he was for a time a professor of music.

Aaron Copland also became my friend during my early days at Tanglewood. Every summer a distinguished guest composer taught composition, and Copland did that. He took a special interest in the students. I remember driving around Tanglewood in my car and seeing Copland on the road. He stopped me and I thought he wanted a ride, but he just leaned in the window and talked to me ten or fifteen minutes about what I was doing and what I was interested in accomplishing.

Riders to the Sea was not the first opera I conducted. The first opera I conducted was at the Settlement House in Boston, at the Peabody Playhouse. It was *The Bartered Bride* by Czech composer

Bedřich Smetana. Boris Goldovsky was asked to suggest some-body to produce a performance there. As he was engaged to stage *The Bartered Bride* in Providence, and to conduct it, he decided it would be nice for me to do it at the Peabody Playhouse. He in-structed me and gave me the staging for the whole opera. I simply did his blockings and used his production, but I did it by myself. I used many of the same performers he used. It was a wonderful experience.

In Providence there was a lovely little conservatory. Maurice Lewis was the conductor there. He liked me when I worked as Boris's assistant. The next year I was engaged to come down one day a week to Providence to teach an opera class. I got my plane ticket, a wonderful dinner (his wife was a marvelous cook), and returned to Boston the same night. I was paid ten dollars a week.

When Goldovsky arranged for me to be on the faculty of the opera department of the conservatory, my salary rose most com-fortingly. I felt independent at last. I had other part-time jobs in addition. I was teaching opera both at the Longy School in Cam-bridge and at Boston University.

My association with Boston University did not just enable me to become more financially independent; it also furnished the pos-sibility of producing two operas that were very important to me.

While I was at Boston University I produced Mozart's little-known opera, *La finta giardiniera* and Stravinsky's *The Rake's Progress.* Both were student performances. As I became busy with productions there, my own methods of presentation evolved, and a cooling-off of my artistic dependence on Goldovsky began to develop.

At Goldovsky's suggestion we took *La finta giardiniera,* an opera written by Mozart when he was eighteen years old, to Tangle-wood, where Goldovsky was head of the opera department. I was his assistant. The version we presented was expanded, and at Tan-glewood it was a big hit. As a result, I was invited to conduct it in the old Boston Opera House on Huntington Avenue, and that became my debut as a professional conductor.

When the opera was a success in Boston, it was decided that Goldovsky's New England Opera Theater would tour it. This would be the first opportunity for one of my opera productions to be performed beyond Boston and Tanglewood. It traveled, but I didn't, and I did not get credit on the program even though it was my production.

I was told that audiences would not accept a woman conductor, and I wasn't allowed to go along. I can understand now that they didn't want a disgruntled Sarah on that trip. I understood it then, but I was annoyed and I felt betrayed. I couldn't believe they didn't let me do it because I was a woman!

La finta giardiniera is a comic opera set in Italy in the mid-eighteenth century. There's a lady, Sandrina, in disguise. She is falsely thought to be a gardener but she turns out to be a great lady. There are some wonderfully funny situations. The Mayor of Lagonero sings an aria about his family tree and he's got one growing in the garden.

There's a delightful aria that the leading tenor, Count Belfiore, sings when he is about to meet the wife whom he believes dead. He thinks that he has killed her but he hasn't. He is relaxing in the garden. He says, "It's a beautiful day. The flutes and the oboes are playing. Oh! That modulation! The violas are playing, the bassoons—what are they trying to tell me?" He goes down to the orchestra pit to receive the musical message, the warning that his wife is about to approach.

The young baritone, Nardo, who is in love with the maid, Serpetta, sings of his love for her. She tells him, "If you want to make love to me you must sing an aria, and you must sing in a foreign language." So he sings a little aria with sections in German, in French, and in English. That was the only time Mozart wrote for the operatic stage in English.

My production of Vaughan Williams's *Riders to the Sea* at Tanglewood earlier had caught the attention of Koussevitzky, who invited me to be a member of the Tanglewood teaching staff. I worked very hard on that production. Once, when I was in the theater alone, I stepped backward and fell off the stage into the pit. I picked myself up, hitchhiked to Lenox, where I received emergency treatment for my sprained wrist at a clinic, and made my way back in time for a rehearsal that evening.

The first season I was there as a teacher, one of the opera designers did not have the sets ready in time to do enough rehearsals. At the end of the season he was fired. But he was fired in a grand way. The whole faculty was called to a meeting and Koussevitzky got up and announced that he had fired that person because he had not given 200 percent. Because it was such an incredible privilege to be there, it was necessary, Koussevitzky stated, for everyone who was in Tanglewood to give 200 percent. We were warned that anyone who did not give 200 percent knew what awaited.

There was a suspicion that Henrietta Hirshman, a lovely Russian lady who was Koussevitzky's secretary, kept track of faculty who came and did not come to concerts. Not everybody on the faculty went to every concert but most did go backstage after the concerts. Haunted by the fear that my appointment might have been a mistake, I had worked wildly that summer, rehearsing almost every night. I was staging Lenny Bernstein's *Trouble in Tahiti,* an opera that would not have its professional premiere until 1952.

Finally, when the opera season was over, I did go to a concert. Boris Goldovsky told me that I should go backstage, so I went backstage. To my amazement, Koussevitzky walked over to me and said, "Caldvell, How nice to see you at a concert!" and I thought, "That's the end of me."

The next afternoon I again went backstage, having convinced myself that his comment was just an accident, that "Genrietta Girshman," as Koussevitzky called her with his incomparable Russian accent, did not really take roll after all. This time I was greeted by Koussevitzky with, "So, Caldvell, you have come to another concert!"

Each year, on the last Sunday night of the season, Koussevitzky gave a dinner for the faculty. As I went to my first faculty dinner at the Curtis Hotel, I wondered, "Would it also be my last?" I thought, "I've got to do something!"

I saw that Koussevitzky, elegant in all white, was surrounded by the usual group of Tanglewood admirers. I went up to him, my heart pounding, and said, "Dr. Koussevitzky, there's just one thing wrong with Tanglewood!" Surprised, and indignant, he asked, "Oh!? And vat is vrrong with Tonglevood?" I replied that I hadn't figured out a way to give 200 percent and still go to every concert. There was a moment of terrible silence and then he announced for everyone to hear: "I never vant to see you at another concert!" Then he hugged me.

I could relax then, and enjoy the first steak tartare I had ever had in my life. It was divine.

Koussevitzky had a unique way of running his life and his orchestra. No one told him what to play. He called his board his "trusties." If he wanted something to happen and his trusties didn't support him, he would simply threaten to resign, or he *would* resign. Then they would come to him and beg him not to resign and work it out somehow.

Koussevitzky had been willed the grounds and buildings of Tanglewood by two devoted lady benefactors. He was the emperor of the earth until he did something not well thought out. He gave Tanglewood to the Boston Symphony.

Soon after, he wanted something the board wouldn't agree to, so as usual, Koussevitzky resigned. It was rumored that he insisted upon engaging Leonard Bernstein as his co-conductor and his heir apparent but the board did not fancy this brash young Jewish upstart as Koussevitzky's successor. The next morning Koussevitzky read in the paper that his resignation had been accepted.

He continued, though, to be music director at Tanglewood.

Chapter 10

The Opera Group

After a time, Boris Goldovsky's New England Opera Theater began dwindling away. Finally it was reduced to playing only one sad production of *Don Giovanni.* During that time I approached Goldovsky with a plan designed to rejuvenate the New England Opera Theater. Together with a young man who was a public relations executive, Charles Forester, we had developed it to try to help preserve the company.

Charles Forester, a baritone, had been studying opera in my evening opera class. After class we would go out and talk about what could make opera work best. He felt that the New England Opera Theater could be brought back to life by a public relations campaign. We agreed that in a country where you could sell green toothpaste, you could certainly sell opera and operated on that assumption.

Perhaps because Goldovsky was tired or disconcerted or he didn't have faith in our ability to do what we wanted to do, instead of taking our plan seriously, he suggested that I organize something of my own. I decided to do just that, and formed the Opera Group.

Charles Forester masterminded the development of a big public relations campaign for us. We wrote a prospectus for establishing a new opera company. Goldovsky endorsed it and sent me to several of his supporters, who gave us a little money—a few hundred dollars. I went to Madame Koussevitzky (her husband having died in 1951) and, at Goldovsky's suggestion, she wrote a beautiful letter that we included in our prospectus.

When we announced an opera season, Goldovsky's supporters woke up to what we were doing and they were very displeased. Goldovsky himself wrote a letter to everyone on his subscribers' list denouncing our efforts and disassociating himself from us. He told us that he simply had to do that. I suspected he had been given an ultimatum by the major supporters that he still retained. In this letter he stated that he was sure we were planning to do productions with reduced orchestra and incomplete sets and he did not approve of that. Considering that he had toured with reduced orchestra and incomplete sets, this was surprising criticism from him.

The results were interesting. Our supporters were furious. They thought it was in very poor taste and it galvanized them in a way that nothing else could have done. As we continued our campaign we had a big display of posters and pictures where people came to buy subscriptions. Goldovsky's supporters came to protest. One lady burst into tears and had to be taken away.

Charlie Forester was a brilliant entrepreneur and promoter but a less brilliant businessman—or at least that was the perception. Our board wanted us to get a different manager. Eventually Charlie was removed by the board. Unfortunately, he died shortly thereafter. I think of him a lot. I wish that he were around to do it again.

There was a big birthday party planned for Goldovsky by the guild of his company, and by some mistake I was invited. At this point nobody of his group was speaking to me. I called and said, "I would like to bring to the party as a gift a list of the nine thousand new opera fans we have recruited." I don't know whether Boris ever knew about this, but both his wife and the head of his board called and said that they would rather I didn't come. So I didn't go, and they never got the list.

With encouragement from Community Concerts, the organization that had helped us develop our list of subscribers, we decided that we should branch out, continuing to use their recruiting method.

With money we had received from a foundation grant we engaged a professional organizer who went from town to town and organized committees. He came back and suggested the places he thought would be productive. For Winchester, Wellesley, and Cambridge (all in Massachusetts), we produced Puccini's *Madama Butterfly.*

I went to the famous scene designer Jo Mielziner in New York to ask for his assistance. He said he was too busy to do it but he recommended a young Chinese set designer named Ming Cho Lee, a man who has since become one of the best stage designers in this country. He designed a beautiful set, one I still love more than any other Butterfly set I know.

Before talking with Ming, I did a lot of research on the kind of environment I wanted. I read books on life in Japan at the turn of the century. I studied sketches of everything from eating utensils to furnishings to the whole way of life—clothes, everything. I wanted the set to be as simple and realistic as it could be, not glitzy and romantically unreal. Ming and I talked a great deal and I showed him books, and he had a lot more books and we talked more. He designed the most versatile and appropriate set for *Madama Butterfly* I have ever seen.

A small Japanese house is set in the midst of a bamboo grove. In the back there's a bridge that leads up a hill and goes over a small stream. Downstage toward the conductor there is a little garden. The house has shoji screens that open and close. The colors are beige, brown, and the very pale waxy color of bamboo. As the sets were designed for touring, they did not have to be rigged.

The lighting sequence was the most famous part of the play by David Belasco. Puccini saw the play *Madama Butterfly,* in London, and he was so impressed by it he asked Belasco's permission to use it as the basis for an opera. He was enchanted by the lighting sequence during which Butterfly stands waiting all through the night for Pinkerton to return. Puccini composed what is called his "Lighting Symphony," a long, long beautiful orchestra interlude in which the lighting on the stage goes from sunset, to dusk, to night, through various phases of night through dawn and ends with the rising sun.

When the opera was performed in 1904 in Italy, the original two acts as it was written were divided into three acts, using a shortened symphony to end the second act and begin the third.

In our productions of *Madama Butterfly* we brought the three acts back into two. It was difficult for us to do but we did it. Fortunately at Ricordi (the publisher of Puccini) in Milan, Osbourne McConathy was allowed to study the original score. He was able to restore parts of the opera as it was originally written. Ricordi has consistently been helpful when we have tried to find music that had been cut when we wanted to use it in our productions.

Included were some very interesting variations. More chorus scenes in the first act gave us an opportunity to see the Japanese family of Cio-Cio-San and the Japanese population making fun of and mocking Pinkerton, and Sharpless, and the Americans. At the same time the Americans were laughing at the Japanese. Those were wonderful moments.

The first performing score also included an aria for Cio-Cio-San's drunken uncle, Yakusidé, in which he embarrassed himself and the Japanese a bit. Some beautiful sections of the love duet between Cio-Cio-San and Pinkerton were reinstated.

In the revised version, Pinkerton has an aria because tenors insist on having an aria; originally, however, there was a trio with Pinkerton, Kate Pinkerton, and Suzuki. It's a very beautiful, distinguished, and wonderful piece. It's very touching. I think the opera is better without the tenor's aria but I have yet to find a tenor who agrees with me. But there are ways of combining both, and I must admit that I have allowed tenors to sing the aria and do the trio as well.

Almost everyone in our first cast for *Madama Butterfly*, except of course for Pinkerton and Sharpless, and Kate Pinterton—was oriental. Our original Cio-Cio-San was Taeko Tsukamoto, Pinkerton was Thomas Hawyard, and Sharpless was John Reardon. We had a very highly educated chorus including doctors, doctoral candidates, and undergraduates at Harvard and MIT.

We had a Japanese flower-arranging expert help us, and we had a Japanese choreographer arrange the dancing at the wedding. He played a tiny role in the piece. One night during rehearsal he called the cast together, stood up on a box, and denounced America in highly broken English. He disappeared before we had a chance to respond.

We have had many exceptional singers sing the part of Cio-Cio-San. One of the best was Sarah Reese, who is black. Made up to appear pale, her gentleness and warmth made you believe in her. One of our Cio-Cio-San's was an Hungarian soprano, Veronica Kinces, a lovely artist who later sang the part in Europe. A recording of the opera in which she sang won the gold Prix du Disque.

In the course of the years we have done many performances of *Butterfly*. The set is as beautiful today as it was more than thirty-five years ago.

Chapter 11

The American National Opera

There was a touring company run by a famous singer, Risë Stevens, called the Metropolitan National Company, which showcased young American singers. It was toured by impresario Sol Hurok. Although it was well underwritten, they stopped performing for a variety of reasons unspecified (at least to me).

Roger Stevens, chairman for the National Endowment for the Arts, called me. He came to Boston and asked if I would consider forming a touring company that would be blessed by the Metropolitan Opera. He said that Hurok had the tour booked for the whole next year.

It was summertime and I was flown in a private plane to the Hamptons on Long Island, where the Metropolitan was giving a concert. The plane landed. There was a helicopter that took me to meet with Rudolf Bing, who was then general manager of the Metropolitan Opera.

The purpose of this visit was for Bing to decide whether or not he and I could work together. He made it clear that if I were to become the artistic director of the traveling company that was a branch of the Metropolitan that *he*, Rudolf Bing, would be the overall artistic director and I would report to him.

"Tell me what your ideas are," he said. I talked for ten minutes, outlining plans for the next two or three years if this indeed were to happen. I confessed that I was concerned that I might not have sufficient artistic freedom. Then he said, "I approve of everything.

It's OK. We don't have to talk any more. Just do it." I thought that was wonderful, and I agreed to do the tour.

I wanted to have a year to plan and revitalize the company and I wanted to postpone touring for that reason but Sol Hurok wouldn't stand for it. He claimed to have already booked the tour.

When we went on the tour of what was by then called the American National Opera, we discovered that it was only partially booked. The weekly income was often not sufficient to pay the bills. Every Friday we had to meet a payroll. On Saturday I would have to start trying all over again to raise enough money to meet the next week's payroll. Although there were estimates, often far less money came in.

Sometimes we would give one, sometimes two or three performances. It was a nightmare, but we survived it. It was exhausting, but everyone got paid. *I* didn't, but at that moment it did not seem important. It was an experience that taught me that you have to organize things carefully and that you can't just take someone's word for what will happen.

Touring doesn't have to be deadly. It can give the productions the possibility of becoming better and better, if the conditions for the performers are appropriate.

The art of the singing actor requires the expenditure of a remarkable amount of physical energy. It is necessary to sing and to act at the same time. The performer must be in excellent health. This was not always the case with our company but we did our best. We once had a performance of *Carmen* that required three tenors to complete. Almost everyone in the company had come down with a virus. None of our tenors could last more than one act. The audience was intrigued but it did not enhance the opera. Still, we were proud to prove that we could do it.

In addition to *Carmen*, we performed *Tosca*, *Lulu*, and *Falstaff* and received excellent reviews for all of them. By far the most noteworthy—and controversial—of our productions was *The Rake's*

Progress, which we staged with the assistance and approval of the composer himself, Igor Stravinsky.

The *Rake's Progress* we took on tour was the third production of that opera on which I had worked. The first was a student production that was produced while I was teaching at Boston University. We had a wonderful dean, Robert Choate, who asked me, "What would you like to do?" I said I'd like to do *The Rake's Progress.* In 1951 it had just had its premiere in Venice. I said I would like to invite Stravinsky himself to conduct it. Dean Choate said, "Let's do it!" and wrote to Stravinsky. After a lot of negotiation he accepted.

Before our student production was ready, the Metropolitan Opera held the American premiere. Dean Choate—God bless him!—sent me to live in New York for about six weeks at the Gladstone Hotel where the Stravinskys were staying. After a few days, I was greatly welcomed by Stravinsky's entourage because I would take him to rehearsals, and that left them free to do other things. Igor Stravinsky and I had lunch together every day and we became friends.

It was fascinating to me to see how Stravinsky, like Koussevitzky, created an atmosphere in which one had the feeling that the most important thing on earth in music was happening at that moment right there.

Our student production at Boston University was carefully put together. Stravinsky liked the production and seemed to be much moved by it—and, of course, it provided an incredible experience for the students.

In contrast, he hated the Metropolitan Opera production. He didn't just dislike it; he despised it. He said he thought the sets were unbelievably ugly because they were so literal and not at all contemporary in feeling. When Horace Armistead, who designed the production, later came to Boston, we became friends and Armistead confided to me, "You know, I can't tell you what an awful experience it was working with Stravinsky. I wanted to design something modern but I had to turn out sets which were quite literal, which I hated, because they were what Stravinsky said he wanted!"

When we planned our production at Boston University I had Robert O'Hearn, our scenic designer, bring his portfolio for Stravinsky to look at. O'Hearn had created designs in many styles in the numerous productions he had designed. Stravinsky looked through the sketches and photographs in the portfolio and said, "That is the brothel scene! This is the graveyard scene!" We worked our way through the portfolio and when we got to things Stravinsky didn't like, they helped O'Hearn develop a sense of what would please Stravinsky. O'Hearn did two or three sketches for each scene. Each one was a little different, and Stravinsky selected the ones he liked without verbal discussion.

Several years later we did *The Rake's Progress* again with Stravinsky's collaboration. It evolved into a "mod" production and was one of the most exciting things I have ever experienced. We performed it first in Boston, we toured the country with it for the American National Opera Company, and we took it to Los Angeles where Stravinsky lived.

When we started talking with the set designers, Herbert Senn and Helen Pond, one of them said, "Oh, dear. This is just a sweet old-fashioned opera. Why do we have to do this?" I got angry, because I knew it was neither sweet nor old-fashioned. When I finished arguing with them, telling them what I thought the piece was about, they said, "Why don't we try to do it in a way that makes that clear?"

This was the time of Timothy Leary and his psychedelic celebrations. We went down to the Village in New York, where Leary was doing a New York version of his California psychedelic extravaganzas. We saw wonderful projections that changed the interior of the theater. The music was intrusive and intimate, and there were flashing lights in our eyes from the projections.

Later we took Stravinsky to a discotheque and he was enraptured. The flashing lights, the loud music, the projections—he found it all exciting, the most exciting things, he said, he had seen or heard in years.

Then we began talking about a contemporary setting for *The Rake's Progress* as a metaphor for our times. Stravinsky approved the idea. He proposed setting the brothel scene in a discotheque and stipulated that Tom Rakewell, the hero, sing an aria into a microphone. Stravinsky was insistent that the brothel have flashing lights directed into the audience's eyes. The later scene, in the graveyard became an automobile graveyard. In the first scene, Tom Rakewell was working on his motorcycle; in the last scene, in Bedlam, he was lying near his motorcycle, which was bandaged in all the white adhesive tape we could find.

Herbert Senn and Helen Pond paid their respects to Hogarth by making each piece of scenery look like a black-and-white engraving. Some of the costumes were black and white, but some of them, depending on the situation, were brilliantly colored.

While we were preparing the production in Boston, Stravinsky, who was not well enough to come, was constantly on the telephone, asking how things were progressing. Robert Craft, his alter ego, was especially helpful to us during the evolution of the production.

When we took *The Rake's Progress* to Arizona for further rehearsal before California, Stravinsky did come. He said he did not want to upset the performers so he would be an anonymous spectator at the dress rehearsal. To achieve this he wore dark glasses. Of course because of his profile everyone knew who he was.

When we got to the brothel scene, I noticed that he began scowling. At the intermission I said "Okay, Papa"(everyone called him Papa), "What is it? You're not happy. Tell me why." What was wrong was that the sound enhancement was not loud enough. He wanted, he expected, the theater to rock with sound as it had when he visited the discotheque.

For the Los Angeles performance we rented every available piece of amplification equipment we could get out hands on, but it still wasn't loud enough to suit the composer. You can't make a big theater shake like you can a small room.

The men in the chorus in the brothel scene were dressed in dark blue and wore white shirts with white collars and cuffs with big white flowers printed all over them. Stravinsky wanted such a shirt himself. Helen Pond went out to find Stravinsky a shirt to decorate and had finally to go to a boys' store to buy one because he was diminutive.

Although Stravinsky came to the dress rehearsal and seemed quite happy with what he saw and heard, he did not feel well and did not come to the opening night performance. The next day, we were crushed by the press, receiving the worst reviews we had ever gotten. Basically they said, "Who does she think she is to desecrate this beautiful opera by producing it in such a way!"

Stravinsky told the press the following day that this was the most beautiful production of his opera he had ever seen and the one he preferred.

This was an important lesson to me. If I had shared with the press information about what to expect, and the fact that Stravinsky had been involved in every detail, they probably would have covered it very differently.

That was a time when we changed things, but we changed things for a reason. We didn't do it to be different. We did it to try to restore the immediacy that the opera had originally.

The American National Opera Company lasted only one year but we had a great time during that year. Sol Hurok wanted to continue, and so did I, but the additional money that would have been necessary to make that possible was not forthcoming.

Chapter 12

New York City

Through the years New York has been the venue for unexpected happenings more often than most other places. Boston has served up its share of excitement; in retrospect, however, that excitement was usually predictable.

I first started going to New York as Boris Goldovsky's assistant to help with a televised version of *Carmen* which he conducted. Soon I was helping write *Opera News on the Air* scripts for the Saturday afternoon radio broadcasts. When a script I had worked on was played, I was invited to the Metropolitan broadcast and invited to lunch by Texaco. I also got to sit in on the intermission broadcast. That was very important to me as I was still a student.

At one of those broadcasts, Mary Garden was a guest. She was very old, and she was wearing a brilliant red suit. There was a pitcher of ice water in the room. When she asked for water, I picked up the pitcher, and as she said, "Hurry! Hurry!" I moved toward her. When she repeated impatiently, "Hurry, girl, hurry!" I became so flustered I spilled the contents of the pitcher all over her. She was of course quite startled. Suddenly there were a dozen men with a dozen white handkerchiefs trying to dry her off and pick up the ice cubes.

Almost immediately, soaking wet in her bright red suit, she went on the air and spoke with perfect composure.

Many years later there was a month when my picture was on the cover of the magazine section of the *New York Times, Musical*

America, and *Time* magazine. As a result I was invited to do a lot of things in New York and in other cities across America.

My first professional experience in New York was staging and conducting several productions at the New York City Opera. I was the second woman invited to conduct there. I conducted and staged *The Barber of Seville* and *Falstaff,* and staged *Ariadne auf Naxos* by Richard Strauss. Julius Rudel, music director for the New York City Opera Company, conducted.

Rossini's *The Barber of Seville* was the first opera I conducted in New York. We had staged it earlier in Boston. Beverly Sills was amused when I called her and asked her to audition some mechanical birds. We bought a very beautiful mechanical bird in a cage for her bedroom. The set, designed by Herbert Senn and Helen Pond, provided her with a bedroom shaped very much like a bird cage. Beverly sang duets, vocalizing with the mechanical bird.

I staged *Der junge Lord,* by the German composer Hans Werner Henze, and it was also conducted by Julius Rudel. Soon after Rudolf Bing left the Metropolitan Opera as general manager, he agreed to play the nonsinging role of a terribly elegant gentleman. Because he owned dachshunds, we thought it would be fun for him to arrive in his carriage with dachshunds. He wouldn't use his own dogs, but we did get dachshunds, and it worked very nicely. He was a very fine colleague. He attended a lot of rehearsals. He said that he had never seen anything quite like the way we put it together.

I took Kenneth Riegel, who played the part of the young lord who turns out to be an ape, to the zoo to see how apes walked and behaved. He was not pleased with the excursion but I think it did prove to be helpful. At least he learned to scratch very convincingly.

I had the experience of fitting into the way that company operated. Time did not permit fully fleshed-out performances, but I learned a great deal. A lot of the disciplines they had, a lot of the techniques they had, were time-saving and permitted the director to do some interesting things.

I conducted performances of the New York Philharmonic in the Park during some of the summer performances.

During this time, although I was trying to do too many things, I thrived on it. At the same time that I was working at the New York City Opera, I was also conducting at Penn State an American opera called *Be Glad Then, America* by John LaMontaine. Penn State is in a place where you can't get there from anywhere. The president of Penn State had a plane, and the dean of the School of Fine Arts (who was very excited about the project), managed to commandeer the plane to take me back and forth to and from Penn State from New York and from Boston where I also had responsibilities.

While I was conducting at New York City Opera I was given an award by the Carborundum Corporation in upstate New York, a very nice award. I couldn't go to accept it because the banquet was scheduled the same evening as the dress rehearsal for one of the operas I was preparing to conduct at the New York City Opera. Although they offered to send a private plane for me, I couldn't fail to be present at the dress rehearsal.

The Carborundum Corporation people very kindly came to Boston later and made the presentation to me of a very beautiful piece of sculpture. My staff, which was never trained to be completely respectful, referred to it as the "Miss Abrasive of the Year Award."

I conducted the New York Philharmonic in a concert of works by contemporary American women composers. It was a concert sponsored by Ms. magazine, a feminist magazine, in support of their pension fund.

I had the responsibility of deciding what the program would be. They sent me a lot of music by women composers. I got all kinds of tapes and scores, and the house was full of ladies' music.

Someone told me that in Boston there was a lady composer who taught at the conservatory. I called her and she came over with a tape machine and tapes. It was a terribly hot day. She arrived wearing overalls, like the kind mechanics wear. When she connected the tape machine, the tape broke, and she burst into tears, whereupon my little white dog, Cranberry, went over and licked her face. He was very nice to her.

She had written several things including a "piece at random." To accomplish that, you cut up a lot of tapes. You glue them together, having no idea what is on them, and you play them as if you had composed something. She had written such a piece for strings without any measure bars. At the time, that was a rather chic device. I had her score and I decided we could do that at the Philharmonic.

I was as well prepared at the first rehearsal as anybody could have been. The piece for strings had different entrances for perhaps as many as thirteen different violinists. I had a stopwatch and told the violinists that they would have a certain number of seconds to play the music and they were all to play at once.

I knew the sequence in which the violinists were supposed to come in. I had practiced it a zillion times with chairs lined up, so I knew I could do it with confidence. In fact I expected to do it with a great deal of pizzazz.

The violins at the Philharmonic were not used to this system of being pointed to, so they complained bitterly. They didn't want to do it, so I said, "This is short and simple, and I really know it very well, fellows!" It made them nervous, nevertheless.

The composer was there, and after the rehearsal she insisted that they wouldn't play her piece because they were against her personally. I said, "We can set this up with measure bars. We can write out the music and make a score and fix it so it will come out exactly the same way so they won't be playing 129 notes without measure bars. Rather than doing it horizontally, we can do it vertically so it will look like music they are used to playing."

"No," she said, "there isn't time." And I said, "We can do it before tomorrow." I had an assistant who went off and called a couple of music copyists. With their help, those music parts were produced by the next morning.

It was lots more fun the original way, but at the next session the Philharmonic played it with the score. It was a nice piece, although, as expected, it sounded a little weird.

The composer didn't thank me. She was furious that I had notated it differently and that it came out sounding the way she had written it. It was humiliating to her that I had, in her mind, altered her music. I had done that, granted, but I was trying to save her piece for the concert. I think she would have loved to go around saying that it was so difficult the Philharmonic couldn't play it or that it was too difficult for Sarah Caldwell to conduct.

We tried to play a very fine string quartet by another lady composer. I wanted the whole string section to play because she had written that she wanted them all to play. It was so confusing they couldn't play it. The sequence of notes was too difficult for them. They came to me and said, "We'd love to play it but we can't in the time we have. If we had had the parts for three or four weeks so we could practice them at home it would have been possible." So that string quartet we didn't play.

The pièce de résistance was a clarinet concerto by Thea Musgrave, a Scottish lady composer who later moved to America. It was a very elaborate, very complicated piece. It was played by the first clarinet of the Philharmonic, the extraordinary Stanley Drucker.

After we rehearsed it, Stanley referred to it as "The Fastest Gun in the East" because it had such fast tempos and he had to play so many notes so rapidly.

When I agreed to conduct *La Traviata* at the Metropolitan Opera in 1976, they were having a terrible time with the intonation of the orchestra and were being criticized all over the place. At that time it was considered sinful and just impossible to use any kind of amplification. Although it was not admitted, we knew that in some theaters, just as we were doing, amplification was being used.

Occasionally, depending on the piece and the singers and the set, and various other factors, we amplified the sound of the singers' voices slightly—never to the point that anyone knew it, that it distorted anything, or that it sounded amplified. We called it "sound enhancement" and we listed the sound engineer in our program.

We had a very sensitive sound engineer, Gary Harris, who set up the controls. After two or three rehearsals, because of the relationship of the singer and the orchestra, always bringing these together, he knew where the sound might need a little boost. It was his artistry and sensitivity that has made the use of sound amplification successful.

I gave a rather long radio interview regarding the question of sound and how amplification can best be used. I discussed a device we had brought from Frankfurt some years earlier, something that was then new. It was a head, carved in plastic foam made to look like a human head and in the ears it had places for earphones. If the sound engineer could not be in the hall to test it he recorded on tape what was coming through those ears, as if it were coming through human ears. He would listen to that sound and that was what he would adjust from. It was novel then, although later such a system became relatively well known.

I got to the Metropolitan and three musicians came as a delegation from the orchestra, and said, "We have heard what you do in Boston about amplifying sound from one end of the pit to the other, and that it solves intonation problems, and we would like to have it here. Could you arrange to get it for us?"

I said "Sure," and then began a long series of negotiations with the management. By then Rudolf Bing was no longer at the house. In any event, over a period of about three weeks we held negotiations, sometimes daily. At first when I explained what I wanted to the representative of the management, he said, "It's absolutely impossible! The press would crucify us." I said, "No they won't. You're not amplifying singers' voices. You are not trying to fool anybody. Let's bring them in and show them what we're doing, and explain what the situation is." "Oooooooh!" was the reaction.

I was told that Rudolf Bing had arranged seating in the orchestra and they had made a number of tests and that was the way it was going to be and seating couldn't be changed and there wouldn't be any amplification because he swore that there never would be any amplification in the theater.

I said, "Mr. Bing is no longer here, he doesn't work here any more, and, second, he's my friend, and I'll bring a note from Mr. Bing." We tried that, but then they said there was a difference in the amplification we hadn't discussed.

Eventually, their reply was, "It would cost us a lot of money. We would have to buy all of the equipment." I said, "I would love to make a gift of this equipment." It was very inexpensive and simple. So they went away with that proposition. They came back the next day and said, "It's not possible. It was very generous of you to offer this gift, but we cannot accept it because we would have to engage two stagehands."

I said, "Why?" and the answer was, "They would have to sit in the pit each night when you are conducting. And then they would have to run it." And I said, "No, they wouldn't have to run it. The musicians would control it themselves." "Oooooh! We would never let a musician run a sound system," was the response.

"Well," I countered, "we've done it for many years, often with less talented musicians than you have in your pit and there has never been an accident." In the end the use of sound enhancement was totally vetoed and the orchestra was disappointed and unhappy.

But then, as a compromise, they let me reseat the orchestra. In hearing pitches, you automatically adjust your sense of intonation by the bass note, or the bass sound. If I am the conductor and I am in the pit, and I can get the continuity of the bass instruments, then this helps bring everyone in the orchestra in line. If you have double basses and contrabassoons and bass violins and trombones and all the low instruments positioned so they can hear each other well, you have the best control of intonation. They finally let me do that. As a result we had fine intonation.

Unlike our experience at the Metropolitan, when I did *La Traviata* in Boston with Beverly Sills, we had a long time to rehearse. We had carefully worked out sets. We had several weeks of rehearsal and used orchestra parts that had been researched by Osbourne McConathy in Milan. We went back to the original score.

I also conducted *Elixir of Love* at the Metropolitan. That was a miserable experience for me, even though Luciano Pavarotti was in it as was José Carreras.

My first performance at Carnegie Hall was, in comparison with other musical experiences in New York, sedate and orderly. My conducting debut at Carnegie Hall validated for my mother my decision to conduct rather than to perform, a decision that had been difficult for her and my father to accept.

We presented a concert version of Prokofiev's *War and Peace* based on the operatic version which we had performed in Boston.

Chapter 13

Around America

My performance at Carnegie Hall led to invitations to be guest conductor for orchestras in cities across America. I conducted the concert version of *War and Peace*—excerpts from the opera that we had presented in its American premiere at the Orpheum Theater in Boston—in several cities including Philadelphia, San Antonio, and Cleveland. With me I took thirteen performing artists.

Today there are conductors who will go to the Cleveland Orchestra Library to see what George Szell did to the Schumann symphonies and it is only by luck that anyone has recently heard a Schumann symphony with Schumann's scoring. I had conducted all of the Schumann symphonies the way Schumann wrote them. It was amazing how different they sounded.

Not so many years ago, it became very important to conduct Beethoven like George Szell. He changed every piece that Beethoven wrote in terms of what was to be doubled and what wasn't to be doubled.

When it became fashionable to use period instruments, a number of recording groups in Europe recorded Beethoven symphonies using the kind of horns and the kinds of strings that Beethoven used. The sounds are somewhat different from the ones we hear today.

I had an interesting experience dealing with Beethoven's Ninth Symphony. I happened to have access to the facsimile of the original manuscript and a lot of letters that were written around the time Beethoven was working on it. Beethoven fussed a lot about disliking doubling of instruments: if you double the oboe, for example, and have two people playing the music that the oboes play, you lose the individual quality of expression of the solo instrument. It either sounds like a band, or it sounds like a solo oboe. If you double the instruments, you create a sound different from the one the composer intended.

There was a German conductor who wrote a book about all of Beethoven's symphonies. He told how to conduct them. He explained when to double, measure by measure. Everybody believed him and to this day this book is the Bible of people conducting Beethoven.

When I was invited to go to St. Louis to conduct Beethoven's Ninth Symphony, I listened to a number of recordings and I realized that every recording was doubled, including those by Toscanini.

That is because that is the way it is done. Everybody knows you have to double or you cannot balance properly. I decided that in the case of Beethoven's Ninth that probably wasn't true. So when the St. Louis Symphony said to me, "How many extra horns will you need?" I said "None."

Well, they got very excited. They looked at me and said, "Don't you know that it is always doubled?" I said "Yes, I know that it is always doubled. But I have studied the score very carefully and I have studied Beethoven's ideas very carefully and his comments, and I feel there is no reason why it couldn't be balanced without doubling."

We fought over this. The orchestra committee insisted on doubling the players, some eighteen or twenty of them, and that extra winds and brass be hired. I said, "I don't care. I'm not trying to prevent people from working. Go ahead and hire them, but I want to do it at the first two or three rehearsals without any doubling. I believe I can balance it so it will sound cleaner, more musical, and it will be much more interesting. If it doesn't work we'll have these nice men whom you hired there."

At the first rehearsal, I saw that the doublers were sitting in the orchestra. I said to the assistant conductor, "I want them out." We had a big altercation and I said, "I won't conduct until they leave. I don't want them to leave the auditorium. I just want them to go sit and listen." I talked to them. Of course they were all prejudiced against my changes because they would be losing their places.

But we did it. We had two or three rehearsals and the effect was quite clear. The critics liked it. The critics were not aware of this subterranean world of doubling. They didn't know whether it was doubled or not doubled. We didn't make a big thing of it. I just wanted to play it Beethoven's way and to prove that Beethoven was right.

While I was conducting the National Symphony Orchestra in Washington, I found that my friend from Tanglewood days, Aaron Copland, was conducting there at the same time. We were both staying at the Watergate Hotel. We traveled together to some of the rehearsals and performances. He said how nice it was to see me, but it was obvious his mind was going a bit; after a time he said, "Sarah, where are we? Where are we going?" At the rehearsal he was all right. He conducted the performance brilliantly, but sometimes when he talked with people he frightened them.

During one of the summers when I was at Wolf Trap in the Virginia countryside near Washington, I conducted Copland's *Lincoln Portrait* and he narrated it. It was impressive. Then he suggested, "Let's switch!" and we did. The second time he conducted and I was the narrator. It was attention-getting and shook everybody up because we hadn't told people this was going to happen.

I was at Wolf Trap four summers. I conducted and worked at Wolf Trap and then I was named artistic director. I've never quite known how that appointment came about. They had not had someone in that capacity before. I suspect that because I was at the height of a publicity blitz, that they thought having me as artistic director would enhance their reputation. They thought that suddenly, because of my presence, everything they did was going to be considered marvelous, and they would get great publicity. Unfortunately, they wanted to keep on doing exactly the same things they were doing—which weren't marvelous.

Wolf Trap, in comparison with Tanglewood, had a commercial feeling. There were many nice things but there were many very difficult things. As artistic director I had not any authority at all. The people there wanted my name, they wanted my reputation, but they wanted me to simply do as I was told.

Mrs. Shouse, Catherine Filene Shouse, who had donated her farm for the summer performing arts center, I liked very much. She was my friend. What she really wanted, which I didn't realize when I was asked to come make it a "great serious festival," was to make it a "great serious festival" within the framework that she could bring all of her friends, who came every year to do one concert and then have dinner with her. They would all come back, year after year, and they would all get to choose exactly what they wanted to do.

An exception was Van Cliburn who, after many years of silence, came to perform at Wolf Trap. I went to his dressing room to chat with him, and we worked a bit together. He was obviously nervous. He decided not to attend rehearsal. At the time of the performance, he was fine. He played brilliantly. There were no musical problems at all.

Although Mrs. Shouse did not appear to get any older, unfortunately some of the performers did. The saddest was Yehudi Menuhin. He was a famous man who could no longer play the violin as a virtuoso. But he did not know that he could no longer play well. He thought he was doing wonderfully. He was abetted in this fantasy by his wife, who talked about her husband as if he were the only violinist in the world.

I was thrilled when I heard that he would be playing a Mendelssohn concerto that I had played when I was a little kid. He had been my idol then.

We had a special session to make sure everything would be as he wanted it. At the session he talked gibberish and played funny things on the violin. I thought, "What is going to happen?" Then he said, "I want to talk to the strings," and I said, "Please do. They will be honored."

So I said to the orchestra, "Mr. Menuhin has told me that he would like to say a few things to the string players. I've urged him to do this." I didn't want the orchestra to think he was cutting me down. He talked forever. He would talk, and then he would play, and he sounded so dreadful I was about to cry because here was this great musician disintegrating before our eyes.

When time came for the concert, I almost didn't want to do it. Although he played quite a bit better than at the rehearsal, he didn't play well. Nevertheless, he had a huge success. The audience yelled and cheered and stamped, and he got good reviews. I think that the critics didn't want to face reality. Nobody wanted Yehudi Menuhin's concert not to be good, so no one would believe that it was not wonderful.

Beverly Sills was close to Mrs. Shouse. She brought the New York City Opera there one week every year. She wasn't running anything; she was just singing. When I got my job, Beverly said, "I want you to know that we are still going to bring the New York City Opera every year. Don't think you are going to run the opera." That was fine with me. In my opinion, the more opera the better.

There were pressures on Mrs. Shouse from members of her family to have lots of pop concerts. They wanted box office success. There was a manager there when I came who resented my presence very much; before I appeared, he was choosing performers and music to be played, and all of a sudden I was supposed to be doing that. My efforts were undermined all the way. It was continual turmoil.

Mrs. Shouse's son wanted bluegrass weeks and evenings of contemporary popular music. He insisted that Wolf Trap should be for everybody. I didn't make myself popular by saying, "If we are not careful it will be for nobody."

The Wolf Trap administration fought constantly with the National Park Service, which was in charge of the theatrical facility. I got along well with both sides but that didn't endear me to either side. It was a continual hassle with lots of friction.

There was a year that the scheduled operas were canceled. Mrs. Shouse said to me, "Oh, you've just got to bring the Boston Opera because we have to have opera!" I agreed but I shouldn't have done it.

We brought *Aida* and *The Flying Dutchman,* and both worked well until one night there was a terrible storm. It was the night of one of the *Aida* performances. The cast was on the stage, and the chorus was on the stage, when the highway department canceled because they were afraid of what might happen to the traffic in the storm.

Our contract stated that if the cast was dressed and on the stage, and a performance was canceled, we would still get paid. That huge *Aida* cast was not paid. *We* got sued, not Wolf Trap, by the unions. Somehow we managed to pay, but we were never reimbursed, not even for the orchestra, which was in the pit ready to begin.

I spent an entire summer in Washington. I rented a house. I was to get a fee and expenses. I kept careful records of expenses and never could collect a cent. A number of people who worked for Wolf Trap sued because they had had similar experiences. Probably we should have also.

I outlined a festival, a baroque festival. I said, "Let's set aside two weeks." We had some very competent people lined up who agreed to perform, people whom Mrs. Shouse liked, as well as people she didn't know. She said, "Fine, we'll do it next year."

Then she and the lady who took care of her came to Boston and asked me to have lunch. They told me that they had engaged somebody else to do my job, so the baroque festival I had so carefully planned, was off. My replacement lasted a year.

We cooperated more successfully with the Houston Opera Company. I did several things there. They were usually with Beverly Sills and generally repeats of productions we had presented in Boston.

Dallas provided a very different experience. There I conducted Jules Massenet's *Manon*. Larry Kelly, the director of the Dallas Opera, was a very dear friend. He invited me to do a new production there. Then he called and said he was going to do *Manon* and would I please conduct it and let somebody else direct it. This was shortly after he found he was dying of cancer, so I had to say yes and I did go.

It was an entirely new experience. Opera houses work differently. The techniques for putting a production together determine to a very great extent the result. In Dallas I worked with a prompter for the first time. The prompter was an old-fashioned Italian conductor who was very patient with me.

We cooperated with the Dallas Opera Company and the Dallas Opera Company cooperated with us. In 1968 when we were about to present Australian soprano Joan Sutherland in *La Traviata*, she asked if we could use the sets from the Dallas Opera Company. She thought the Zeffirelli sets were incredible.

We arranged to rent the sets and costumes for $10,000 plus the cost of transportation. This was in the Father Queeg days, when we had use of the theater only certain hours of the day. We didn't know when the truck would arrive, whether the bank would be open, and whether the driver would take a regular check. For that reason we had a $10,000 cashier's check drawn up.

When the truck finally arrived, on a Sunday afternoon when banks were closed, the driver didn't know what a cashier's check was. He tore it up and demanded cash.

I went to a supermarket executive for assistance and he had the managers of five or six stores come to his apartment with cash. Because the supermarket manager didn't want the truck coming to his chic apartment house, I had to take the cash to meet the truck driver. All the money had arrived in Stop and Shop bags. The question became, What were we going to put the money in to move it?

I decided that I would meet the driver at the police station. I said, "I'm going to walk out of this building carrying Stop and

Shop bags. It won't create any suspicion. Nobody will suspect me of carrying a lot of money."

The supermarket manager's wife put celery and groceries on top of the bags to give the impression I had been shopping in a big way, and I walked out.

That's how the story got started about Sarah's carrying money around the streets of Boston in paper bags because her creditors demanded cash.

For a while I had a great time with my colleagues who were running opera companies. We all belonged to Opera America, an organization of American opera directors of which I was vice president. We got together and we became great friends.

The organization made us aware that we shared many problems. Before this organization existed, I felt personally responsible for so many failures—mainly failures to raise enough money, and failures to sell enough tickets. I felt that if I could have just been smarter, or worked another hour each day, or done something differently, I could have made things better. It was therefore a comforting experience to go to meetings with ten or twelve colleagues and discover that if I was having trouble with subscriptions that year, they all were too. If I had trouble raising guild money as small contributions, they were having similar trouble too. If I had trouble finding tenors, everybody was having trouble finding tenors. We would sit for hours and talk about the things that we were doing in trying to solve these problems and we would exchange ideas. We told each other of national sources of money—the Ford Foundation, for example.

Initially, there were eight or ten opera directors who were members. We were administrators, and heads of opera companies. Oddly enough, very few of them have changed companies. They stayed with Opera America while it became larger and larger. They still get together but it has become a bureaucratic organization to which I no longer belong.

I realize now, but I didn't realize then, what was happening. While I was building the opera company, the opera company became my persona. I began to lose contact with people in my profession. After I began conducting in New York at the Philharmonic and at the Metropolitan, and began concentrating on performing—and receiving a lot of publicity—I lost touch with my colleagues.

When I became prominent as a conductor and stage director, when my photograph appeared on the cover of national publications (including *Time* magazine in 1975) and I received honorary doctorates, my relationship with my friends in my profession changed. I was going to places like the Komische Oper that many of these people didn't know existed. I was staging in Boston contemporary operas by people like Stravinsky, Nono, and Schoenberg. We did research. Little of this seemed to be going on in other places, at least in a major way.

I became a kind of maverick. I am still to this day known to some as "that funny lady who likes to go to Russia."

If I had it to do over again, I would do it rather differently. Sometimes I have been sarcastic when I should have been gentle and tolerant. Certainly my attention was mixed and stretched and I was sometimes nervous, but basically when I worked with some of my colleagues I was irritable. Today I would have more of a sense of what they were going through and better perspective on what I was going through. For a while I was more concerned with what I was trying to accomplish than with my friends.

McNeil Lowry, head of the Ford Foundation, once said that when he went into a room he could always spot the arts directors because they all appeared to be somewhat wounded. They were too thin or too fat; they smoked too much, or were nervous, because their fund-raising responsibilities weighed so heavily on them.

OUTSIDE THE
UNITED STATES

Most of Sarah's peripatetic musical experiences happened simultaneously with the Boston productions. Invitations to perform took her not only across the United States, but to Canada and to Latin America, as well as to Europe, Africa, and Asia.

Those concerts were primarily of symphonic music. Meticulous in her selection of music for overseas concerts, Sarah avoided when possible what she called "those old chestnuts, the crowd-pleasers." Always included was contemporary music, particularly music from the country in which the performances took place.

As Boris Goldovsky had been her mentor in Boston, Walter Felsenstein became her mentor in Germany. The techniques and philosophy of his Komische Oper in East Berlin determined the nuances her own career would exemplify. That included a sometimes exasperating attention to details. Like Felsenstein, sometimes she postponed or replaced announced operas when details were not absolutely right in her estimation.

Sarah suspected that she was criticized in Boston because of what appeared to be her concern with musical organizations in countries that lacked the political freedom of America, including East Germany, South Africa, China, the Philippines, and most especially, the Soviet Union. She considered communication with people of different nationalities to be the best means of bridging difficulties, and music the ideal method for making friends and bringing about understanding.

Sarah and I met in 1987 in Washington at an exhibition of art from Russian museums. When she learned that I lived in Moscow, where my husband, Jack Matlock, was the American ambassador, she told me that she and Rodion Shchedrin, a composer whom we knew, were arranging a musical exchange between the United States and the Soviet Union.

She exuded such confidence and excitement about the project that I immediately offered to help in any way I could. I told her that she would be welcome to stay with us at the residence, at Spaso House, when she was in Moscow. She came often during negotiations for the festival, which would be called Making Music Together, and for performances in several cities.

She bounced off the plane with enormous energy, ready to work. Nothing deterred her. Once, when her luggage didn't make it to Moscow, she made do with scarves and loopy necklaces that I was able to provide and looked different every day.

Sarah loved to give presents. One of the scarves she borrowed was a Gucci scarf that had been her present to me. It is gold and brown and black and covered with birds. I wear it the first day of autumn each year. She also gave me a dramatic pin that I wear when I wear black. It was designed by her friend, Phyllis Green, who was once a designer for Georg Jensen. Phyllis happened to see me wearing it one day and remarked, "You are wearing Volcano!" Each piece of her jewelry has a name.

I mentioned once in Moscow that whenever I photographed Leonid Pasternak's country house it seemed to be leaning. Sarah presented me with a special lens to take care of that problem. When I went out to Peredelkino, the writers' colony where he had lived, to photograph the Pasternak dacha for the third time, I realized that the house itself was leaning. Her gift made it stand up straight nevertheless.

Once, when she could not attend a reception to which we had invited her, she sent beaten biscuits and country ham to offer to the guests. I haven't been able to open her last gift, lavender honey in a lavender container. It just sits on the pantry shelf to be admired.

I took our grandson, John, when he was still a preschooler, to Boston to see *The Nutcracker* with its extraordinary stage sets by her favorite designers, Helen Pond and Herbert Senn. We stayed with Sarah. Several years later, when John was a teenager, I mentioned that he had become fascinated by jazz. She sent him a complete set of jazz recordings by one of her friends.

When she heard Jack mention that he very much liked Russian mustard, she brought him a jar from Yekaterinburg. Unfortunately, it came open in her suitcase. When I tried to commiserate, she insisted that it didn't matter because it was the same color as her new yellow coat.

Sarah was famous for appearing casual about clothing, particularly when she was working on a new production. The second time I met her was at City Hall in Boston, where she was conducting a rehearsal. Bruce Rossley, who had introduced us originally, asked if I would like to see her again. I said of course I would. Soon in rolled a large gray ball. The conductor was wearing a gray jogging suit, the only time I saw her so attired.

For public appearances she was careful about her clothing. Photographs that I made over several years never showed her wearing the same things. Once, when she wanted an outfit for a special occasion, she had it made by a costume designer.

For performances she liked to have a hairdresser on hand. She was so fond of her Boston hairdresser that when someone who was expected to join us at her table at the American Society of Arts and Letters (when her friend Jill Conway was to lecture) couldn't come at the last minute, she invited him. I sat next to him and enjoyed discussing our mutual enthusiasm for the performances of the singer, Karen Akers, from Washington.

Once, when Sarah had left Moscow to conduct in Saratov, I discovered that her glasses had been left behind. When we finally got through by telephone to suggest sending them by courier, she said it wouldn't be necessary; she traveled with extra pairs of drugstore glasses because she misplaced them so often.

During her time in Moscow, Sarah always remained goal-oriented. Once when I had invited a boys' choir from the closed city of Nizhniy Novgorod to perform at Spaso House to coincide with one of her visits, she didn't hear them perform. That

Yehudi Menuhin and Andrei Sakharov confer at the American ambassador's residence in Moscow

was because she had a request from the Ministry of Culture to go to an unscheduled meeting on a Sunday morning. The young performers were disappointed when they didn't have the opportunity to "audition," but their disappointment was short-lived. That was because we seated them at tables in the Spaso House Gallery and gave them Big Macs, donated by the recently opened McDonald's in Moscow. The only English I heard any of them speak was a collective, "Thank you!" when they tasted American hamburgers for the first time.

When Sarah was staying with us, we included her in whatever social events we were hosting. One memorable night when Jack was out of town, she was there when I entertained Yehudi Menuhin and his wife, who were visiting Moscow. Andrei Sakharov and his wife, Elena Bonner, came to Spaso House for the first time after his release from internal exile in Gorky. Rodion Shchedrin and his wife, the ballerina Maya Plisetskaya, were also guests. The first photograph I made of Sakharov shows him presumably sleeping while Mrs. Menuhin and a woman from the embassy chat across his middle.

He woke up at the suggestion by Yehudi Menuhin that they write a joint letter to Mr. Gorbachev, who was then head of the Communist Party, pleading with him to free from custody a musician whom they both knew. They wrote it on Spaso House stationery that I gave them. I made a photograph of them together, but an even better one of Sarah with Rodion Shchedrin discussing plans for Making Music Together.

When Making Music Together began in Boston, I was invited to attend. I went from Moscow, but didn't inform the State Department because I considered myself attending as a private citizen, not as the wife of the American ambassador in Moscow. Nevertheless, as I entered the Opera House a man sidled up to me and said he was from the FBI. He told me quietly that if I experienced any difficulty I should give a hand signal and help would be available immediately.

Rodion Shchedrin and Sarah Caldwell plan Making Music Together in Moscow

Sarah conducts Aaron Copland's Lincoln Portrait *in Moscow as the American ambassador recites the text in Russian*

Because of Sarah's contacts and those of Shchedrin, the festival in Boston was attended not only by musicians but also by Soviet officials from Moscow and from the Soviet Embassy in Washington, including Ambassador Yuri Dubinin.

At a catered dinner in the Opera House when coffee was served, he asked for tea. The waiter said he was sorry but that tea was not available, whereupon Ambassador Dubinin quipped, "I forgot for a moment that I was in Boston!"

During the return festival, Americans performed in several cities, including Moscow and Leningrad, over a period of two years. Sarah seemed to delight in the complications that travel to distant cities provided. I went to Siberia with her and two American soloists, one of whom took a suitcase full of food. We flew to Akademgorodok, a city neighboring Novosibirsk. It was amazing to see how Sarah made instant friends of musicians, and the audience, without speaking Russian.

She discovered pelmeni, a sort of Siberian ravioli that is considered to be the original frozen food. It is served in masses of sour cream. Sarah announced to the person who was cooking for us that we would like to have pelmeni every night. And we did.

She will tell about the disappointment of not being able to take supporters from Boston as planned because of the first Gulf War in 1991, but will not tell you that she forgot to thank the poet Andrei Voznesensky publicly for translating the dialogue of *The Lincoln Portrait* by Aaron Copland. It was read in Russian by the American ambassador.

There were two other disappointments concerning Making Music Together in the Soviet Union. Leonard Bernstein, who was expected to come and perform his *Mass*, died. The first performance of Making Music Together in Moscow was dedicated to him.

Mikhail Baryshnikov, the ballet dancer who had defected to the United States several years before, agreed to return to dance in his native country, but negotiations with the American Ballet Theatre became so difficult that it could not be arranged.

Sarah inspects a ryijy wall hanging commemorating Making Music Together

Although funding for the performances of Making Music Together in Boston, and in various cities of the Soviet Union, was
difficult to obtain, Sarah persevered. Financial support came from
the State Department, from private businesses, and from other organizations, including the Soros Foundation. But it was never
enough.

Chapter 14

Germany, Israel, and South Africa

My stepfather used to say the most important thing in life is to know who you are and where you are. At different times you are different people and you function differently in different situations. I found that to be absolutely true and very helpful when I traveled abroad.

My first trip to Germany, soon after World War II ended, was to visit Boris Blacher, a German composer whom I had gotten to know in Tanglewood. He set up a composers' tour for me. I went first to Berlin, then to Munich, to visit Carl Orff and Karl Amadeus Hartmann, and on to Salzburg to get acquainted with Gottfried von Einem.

Blacher was infinitely amused by the "cultural enrichment" furnished by the Americans in the aftermath of World War II. The Ford Foundation sent a group of intellectuals to Berlin to stimulate the cultural climate. The Berliners felt they were quite intellectual enough, thank you very much, so there was tension among the community. Even the Ford Foundation people bickered among themselves.

Elliott Carter was there as part of continuing cultural enrichment projects in 1964, as was Roger Sessions. They were entirely different kinds of musicians. Carter did not appear to appreciate opera. His wife, who seemed to dislike all music except her husband's, was there as well. My mother, who sometimes traveled with me, had quite a battle with her because we had a copy of the score of *Montezuma* during its world premiere. Mrs. Carter, seeing this, said, "Oh, let me see!" My mother said, "No, thank you. I am going to follow the score throughout." They got into an argument, and Mrs. Carter said, "Don't be foolish. Let me take it." My mother refused. She wasn't about to give it up.

I always liked to travel with my mother because she was so enthusiastic about being under way. She noticed details and shared her impressions. We always had adventures. She was in a wheelchair because she couldn't walk. It's amazing how much fun you can have with someone in a wheelchair. You get all the service imaginable.

Once, as we landed in Berlin, we looked down and saw an ambulance. My mother said, "Uhh! I bet it's for me. What shall I do?" And it was. Attendants came up and put her on a stretcher. She tried not to be carried away, but they were too strong for her to resist. They carefully took her down the steps, put her in the ambulance, and propelled her to the baggage shed where her wheelchair was waiting.

My mother and I had a memorable trip with Herbert Senn and Helen Pond to East Germany. It was necessary to go through Checkpoint Charlie to cross to East Berlin from West Berlin, where we were staying. Sometimes that took a long time. One night, when we were on our way to the Komische Oper, which was maybe a mile and a half beyond, there were no taxis, and there were no cars on the streets.

We didn't want to be late for the performance, so Herbert Senn ran, pushing my mother in her wheelchair down the middle of the street. While she was having the time of her life, Helen and I were unhappily and unsuccessfully trying to keep up. We got to the Komische Oper without seeing a single car. There we discovered that there was a ban on cars—but presumably not on wheelchairs, because of some kind of alert.

During the early sixties I spent as much time in Germany as I possibly could. I particularly liked to stay in Berlin, where the Austrian opera producer Walter Felsenstein was Intendant at the Komische Oper in East Berlin. In Germany I had one obsession: I wanted to understand how Walter Felsenstein's mind worked, to generate his incomparable productions. I didn't care about anything else.

I met him through a friend, John Moulson, an American tenor who worked at the Komische Oper, and "belonged" to that house. I often stayed with the Moulsons in Berlin, particularly when my mother was not with me.

The first performance I saw by Felsenstein was *Otello*. It was conducted by a young German conductor named Kurt Masur. It was televised and won a prize. It was a beautiful, exciting production, and recordings of it can still be bought today.

The time I spent in Berlin was always centered around the Komische Oper. I basically hung out and attended rehearsals. I had long conversations with Felsenstein and I became very good friends with him and his family.

I saw most of his productions and as many performances of the same operas as I could manage. Felsenstein attended every performance. He would be in his office after the curtain came down and I would go back to get a critique. There was no performance he ever liked. He was a perfectionist. He never believed he could achieve perfection, but, in my opinion, he did. He was a brilliant, brilliant man.

There was a young American director who was studying under Felsenstein. I would have given my right arm to have the chance he did. He complained because he had to work so hard. They were redoing *Otello* and he had to stand in for certain of the actors while the lights were being focused. Felsenstein spent more than three weeks doing this. Instead of complaining, I thought the young man should have been learning why it took so long. He soon got into political trouble and did not become a well-known director.

Felsenstein was an Austrian who had marched to Berlin while he was in the army during World War II. After the war ended, he and his associates petitioned the Americans to allow them to start an opera company. Initially that company was under the supervision of Americans; when the city was partitioned, however, it happened that the theater was in the Russian sector, which was a part of East Germany.

He lived in West Germany but he could go back and forth. His car was never searched, and there was never any political pressure put on him. His theater was totally subsidized by the East German government, leaving him free from financial concerns. This was not because he was secretly collaborating with the Stasi, the East German secret police, but because his theater was the main cultural ornament of East Berlin.

His superb productions were the reason people traveled to East Berlin. Many people were afraid to go to the East, but always there were a few Americans, a few French, and a few British who made it there to see his performances. It was part of Felsenstein's code that the Komische Oper be considered an international house, not just an East German house. We used to say there were three Berlins: East, West, and the Komische Oper.

Walter Felsenstein accomplished more in the theater than anybody else I know. The things that everybody only talks about doing, Felsenstein did. He had a very clear vision of what he wanted to achieve with music theater. He didn't compromise, which meant that the people he used in each opera were absolutely right for that production. He once canceled a performance of *Tales of Hoffmann* because a tenor who had a tiny part was sick.

I would invariably return to Boston full of enthusiasm for what I had learned from observing Walter Felsenstein in action. I tried to share his concepts with my students and with audiences when I staged operas myself.

I was able to arrange for Felsenstein to be invited to Boston University to lecture and to receive an award. A consortium of several area schools supported his visit and held a festival of films of his brilliant opera productions.

I telephoned Boris Goldovsky (with whom I was still, regrettably, not on good terms) and said, "Boris, Walter Felsenstein is here. I told him all about you. I told him how extraordinary you are and how much I learned from you. He would like to meet you. May I bring him out?" Boris answered, "No. You may not bring him out, but if you give him my phone number and he calls me, I'll see him." As it was clear that he did not want me present, I did not pass on the message.

Several years later, I met Boris Goldovsky quite by accident. We were both waiting for transportation after a concert. He was leaning against a wall. I went up to him and asked him if I might telephone him. He said, emphatically, "No!"

I felt that I could not accept that answer from someone who had been so important to me, so I wrote him a long letter describing our relationship of so many years and how important he was to me in my artistic life. I had an answer from his wife thanking me for my letter. I arranged a party at my house that included some of the musicians with whom we both had worked. He came, and was polite to everyone. That was the last time I saw him.

When Walter Felsenstein died in 1975, it was the end of everything. While the Komische Oper is still physically there, and its productions are considered avant-garde, it is in no way Felsenstein's theater. It's very strange to me. Thirty years ago he was held in enormous awe by everybody in the profession. He did the finest productions I heard or saw anywhere, but today very few people know his name.

Upon the recommendation of a German conductor who knew my work, I was invited by the government of Israel to help establish a new Israeli Opera. I felt that I failed miserably—or, rather, the plan that I devised, failed. I went to Israel with my friends Florence and Efraim Margolin, who had an employment agency for professional musical performers in New York. They loved Israel very much and wanted to help.

There was no operatic theater in 1983, but we held auditions. I determined quickly that the caliber of singers in Israel at that time was not high. I was told, nevertheless, that they wanted to present world-class opera. We held workshops for several weeks with singers, stage directors, and directors.

I was given a budget. I said, "All right. Then we must do one or two model productions. We'll take the money we have, and do two beautiful productions."

We constructed plans for *Madama Butterfly*, and for *Don Giovanni*. I asked Ming Cho Lee, the person who designed sets for our *Madama Butterfly*, to design sets to fit in the concert hall. I spoke with two opera performers who were well known in America and explained that we were trying to start something wonderful in Israel and would like for them to sing there.

I said, "We don't have enough money for you to receive your usual fee. If you agree to come, the fee you establish will be the top fee, and we'll then be able to get people from all around the world to come for that fee rather than their usual payment."

Although they were receiving $8,000 and $10,000 for each performance they gave, they both agreed that $2,000 would be their fee. I was very proud of that. I went back to Israel with their commitments.

Soon I was confronted by the mayor and ten or twelve people I'd never met. They were the opera board. They said, "You have committed the entire budget for the production!" And I said, "I have worked within the budget that I was given," and they said, "Oh, no, this is everything. This is money for the educational program, for advertising, and for administration." One of these people then showed me a budget that allowed us about a third of what we had committed.

I objected, saying, "This is impossible!" And they said, "Maybe we don't want these famous people. Why don't you stay over a few weeks and meet with the new manager and work on a program with him?" I was then introduced to the manager of the Jerusalem Orchestra, who was going to be the manager of the company.

I was put up in a place in Jerusalem during Jewish holidays where there was no one with whom I could talk. Deciding that the situation was hopeless, I left for Boston.

Unusual things invariably happened to me when I accepted conducting invitations overseas. During an engagement in Cape Town, South Africa, where I conducted Robert DiDomenica's *The Balcony,* I was asked if I would make a speech before I conducted their symphony orchestra. Although it was a most unusual request, I thought, "Why not?" I made the speech, left the stage, and returned as the conductor.

Once I was invited to conduct in Sweden, in Göteborg. The program, selected by the manager of the orchestra, consisted of two different concerts. I agreed to do both concerts. They were interesting programs. One was a pops concert and one was a subscription concert. They were very nice, very well planned concerts, with music by composers from several countries.

After the second rehearsal, a delegation of ladies called upon me, including the wife of the manager and members of the ladies' guild. They said to me they were proud of the fact that I was the first woman to conduct their orchestra.

They had come, they said, with a request. They informed me that the last guest conductor, when he came out to the podium, looked wonderful because he wore his medals, so would I wear my medals?

Mine is not a country that often bestows medals to wear, and I certainly had not received one. I responded without replying by saying only that I had brought several dresses and I would appreciate their guiding me on what I should wear for the opening concert and reception following. I brought the dresses for them to inspect the next day. Every hem was examined, every label. I thought, "How can I please these nice ladies and not let them down on opening night?"

My mother used to pack for me. She enjoyed it and it was a great help to me. She was always concerned that I might get sick in some strange place and die because they would give me penicillin to which I am wildly allergic. She filled my shoes and my clothes with little pieces of paper that said. "Sarah Caldwell is allergic to penicillin!"

The Christmas before my performance in Sweden, she had given me a large silver medallion, one side of which said, "Sarah Caldwell," while the other side stated, "Allergic to Penecillin" (they misspelled penicillin, much to her great embarrassment). We didn't have it corrected because I thought it was touching.

I looked in my bag. Sure enough, there it was. I went to the local ribbon store and bought several colors of nice ribbon. I wore the black dress the ladies had selected and I wore my medallion. I wore it "Sarah Caldwell"–side out with a certain amount of concern that something might happen and the fact that I was "Allergic to Penecillin" (misspelled), would be announced to everyone, but it didn't.

Chapter 15

The Americas

My first invitation to conduct outside the United States came from Montreal. In Puerto Rico I conducted an all-Bernstein concert.

Once, when I was conducting the National Symphony in Washington, a striking gentleman came to my dressing room. He was wearing striped trousers and various diplomatic decorations, not just one, but three or four or five—quite a collection. He introduced himself with much clicking of heels and kissing of my hand and said he had come in the name of the president to invite me to come to conduct in Venezuela on the occasion of the two-hundredth anniversary of my country, on July 4, 1976.

I was very impressed and gave him the name of my agent. He did indeed contact my agent and an official invitation to Caracas arrived.

Once one has been engaged to conduct, certain negotiations continue: the planning of the program, the details of arrival, "Will you or will you not be willing to make a speech for the ladies' guild?" That kind of thing.

The arrangements in this instance were memorable. The first one came with a phone call, a person-to-person call, from the president. He apparently had little faith in long distance because he was shouting over the phone. Relating to the program, he said, "Is it not true, Madame, that you have in your country a piece that is called "Adagio for Strings?"

"Adagio for Strings" by Samuel Barber is indeed played. And played. And played. And played. It's a nice piece but not necessarily one that I would have chosen. Nonetheless, I said, "Yes, we do," and he said, "Would you play that?" and "We would like to have a program of all-American music in honor of the two hundredth anniversary of your country."

And I said, being polite, "That's a gracious thing for you to suggest, but I would like to include in the program a piece by a Venezuelan composer as well because I think that it would be appropriate. Would you please have something selected and sent to me? Maybe sending two or three pieces would be better." They never appeared.

A little later I got another call. This one was not from the president but from the president's secretary, saying they had had a great disaster. I thought maybe Venezuela had had a revolution or an earthquake, but it hadn't. They had a Mexican violinist whom they had engaged several years earlier to play on the same date and they couldn't get rid of him. Did I mind? He wanted to play Felix Mendelssohn's "Violin Concerto." I mentioned that I had played the "Violin Concerto" myself and that I thought that was fine. We planned the rest of the program.

At one point, from the American Embassy in Caracas, they called to ask if I would bring some Sousa marches. They were afraid that they might not have them in Venezuela. Actually, I almost always take the orchestra music with me; that means I can write little notes and messages to myself on parts ahead of time and save a lot of trouble during rehearsal.

It was a day at the very end of June and it was miserably hot. I got to the airport in Miami and had to wait several hours to get on the plane. We arrived eight or nine hours late, around three or four in the morning.

Friends of friends had assured me that friends of their friends would meet me. As soon as we landed and started inching toward customs, I was warned by other people who had been on the plane that it would take a very long time to get through customs.

Suddenly I heard my name called out. I was ushered through so quickly I didn't know what was happening. The friends of friends of friends obviously had some kind of connections. They spirited me off in their car.

The airport was some distance from the city. On the way in, they asked me casually if I knew there was a kidnap alert out for conductors, and that the last guest conductor had been kidnapped?

I thought to myself, "Well, I don't really know for sure who these friends of friends of friends are, and whether I am actually on the way to my hotel." The fact that I got through customs so quickly began to seem a little sinister. But I was delivered to the hotel without the slightest problem and went to bed in a beautiful room.

The next morning I was surprised to be wakened by the telephone and the voice of the president. Obviously, he had as little faith in the telephone system in Venezuela as he did in the international system because he was still shouting into the phone. The message was that I was welcome to Venezuela and they were looking forward to the concert, but unfortunately the orchestra would not be able to rehearse today because they were going to an island, and that just delivered to my hotel was the music by the Venezuelan composer.

"Going to an island sounds lovely!" I responded, "Could I go too?"

"No, Madame, that would not be possible," he said, with sadness in his voice, "because the orchestra has already left."

It was nine o'clock in the morning. I received the music and quickly determined its structure. It was a tone poem. It had a very even construction. It had phrases that were sixteen measures long and there were sixteen of these phrases. They started softly and made a tremendous build-up in the middle, suddenly dropped down, and kind of did it all over again, except that the ending was quite soft. It was conductor-friendly in that it had very even rhythms that were not particularly notable.

I decided that I would take the piece seriously and I would conduct it from memory. Because it had a pattern, conducting it would not be difficult; it was predictable. The tempo did not change. The dynamics changed at certain places. Harmonically it spoke very easily. There was nothing wild. There were certain phrases for certain instruments that came in for the first time. That was easy to put in my internal computer.

A call came from the American Embassy. I was invited for lunch. I was picked up and taken to a very nice restaurant. It was outdoors where there were a lot of parrots in cages. We were served parrot to eat, which got to me a little bit. When I saw these brightly colored beautiful birds, I somehow wished I weren't eating one. Nevertheless I was up to the challenge.

I asked about the kidnap alert. Up to that point the conversation had been relaxed and friendly but suddenly a pall came over the table. I was told I must not talk about this, but that I was not to be concerned because they were taking care of everything. I was instructed to ride only in embassy cars.

My hosts drove me to the embassy. When they went away to get me some coffee, I managed to find a secretary in another office. From her I learned that there was indeed a kidnap alert but she did not know any details about it. I was quite intrigued by then.

We had coffee, and I was deposited back at the hotel. I was told that an embassy car would pick me up the next morning to go to the rehearsal.

Early the next morning, however, I got a call from the embassy saying I was not to go to the rehearsal. That was because the rehearsal was taking place at the university. The university was Communist, they said, and therefore off-limits to anyone from the embassy. Furthermore, they could not guarantee my safety.

"Look, I'm going to this rehearsal," I insisted, "and I'm not afraid."

Someone from the embassy soon called back and said that one of their drivers was going to go home and change his clothes and drive his own car so he would not be coming as an embassy driver. That way I could go to the university in an unmarked car.

So I went to the university and we had the rehearsal. I was not kidnapped. The only potential disaster was the result of my drinking enormous amounts of tasty papaya juice.

It was an open rehearsal that included the Venezuelan piece. It made a tremendous impression on the orchestra that I took it seriously. I took it so seriously that they declared no one had ever brought out the meaning of this music, the nuances, so well before.

Then we tried some Ives. It was too difficult. They simply couldn't play it. I wasn't sure what to do. I told the orchestra that I realized that they had not had the music long and that we wouldn't rehearse it any more that day. They should take the music home and study it, and we would work on it during the rehearsal the following day.

Someone among the violins said, "You must know that although it may be the custom in your country for musicians to practice at home, we do not have that custom. Nobody can make us take music home and practice. The only rehearsing we do is in the rehearsal."

I answered, "Yes, it is true that in my country that musicians often take music home to practice. I know one thing about all musicians and that is that although they may not be required to take the music home, they take pride in their work and in the way they play. I am sure that since you don't have to, you will take the music home."

He countered, "No!" The next day we tried again to play the Ives score. I suspected that some of the musicians may have practiced at home but it was hopeless to try to play it for the concert.

At the rehearsal I met a charming young girl who was a pianist. The Mexican violinist who had been scheduled for so many years to play this concert had decided not to appear. Instead of Mendelssohn, the young Venezuelan lady said she would like to perform a Schumann piano concerto. I assured her that would be fine with me. She played it very well and we became friends.

She took me for a shopping expedition. I bought some black pearls for my mother, and the young lady's husband, a sculptor, designed a clasp for those black pearls. It was beautiful.

The next day I was taken to lunch by members of the orchestra. They informed me that the concert was scheduled for Sunday morning.

I said, "Why is it, may I ask, that the concert is to be held at such a novel time?"

"We understand that in your country you often have concerts at night," he said, and I assured him that that was true. He explained, "In our country we are the only true democracy south of the United States. We are very much concerned about all kinds of social and political problems. Quite often at the beginning of the week something stirs us up. Everyone becomes involved in it and it turns into what we call 'state of siege.' All the people want to present their views and the matter will grow so that by Friday things are really stirred up, and then on Saturday, a day when everyone is free, we march to demonstrate, but never on Sunday. That's why we schedule our concerts on Sunday so that they do not interfere with 'state of siege.'"

The phrase I heard most often in Venezuela, and I heard it over and over again, was, "This country is the only true democracy south of the United States."

One of the difficulties of being a lady conductor is that you offer more problems to an orchestra than gentlemen conductors ordinarily do. At least I seem to. For example, I like to have a hairdresser at the concert. I went to the hair salon at the hotel to try to arrange for a hairdresser to come to the concert.

I had had my hair done in New York and I thought it looked elegant, with tiny streaks of gray in my dark hair. My new hairstyle had been much complimented by my friends before I left.

I walked into the beauty salon. There were wigs everywhere. Two or three of them were bright, vibrant, orange-red, and a couple of them were black-black-black-black. The hair of all the ladies in the salon was one of those colors. The lady who ran the salon looked at me in horror and said, "You know, Madame, if you wish, we could turn your hair all one color." I did not wish but I did get someone to go with me to the concert.

It had become clear to me that the "trip to the island" had been a euphemism for saying they couldn't find a rehearsal hall. We rehearsed in three different places. I was told that because they were repairing the theater, we couldn't actually go to the theater until the day we performed.

I announced, "I won't perform that way. We must be in at least a day before. I must experience the acoustics and get the feel of the hall." That was eventually arranged and the children from the embassy were invited to the dress rehearsal.

I had been asked to bring music from Mr. Sousa's repertoire. I had rehearsed a Sousa march earlier to try to wipe out the problem of the Ives. I thought it would be easy, but there was resentment. It was obvious that they were uncomfortable playing it.

At the dress rehearsal when we played "The Stars and Stripes Forever," the little kids in the hall got up and danced and waved their arms. Television cameras photographed American children celebrating the American Bicentennial with "The Stars and Stripes Forever" in Venezuela.

The next morning, when I arrived very early in the morning with my hairdresser, I found my friend the pianist and the librarian of the orchestra very upset. The librarian said in anguish, "Madame, the 'Stars and Strippes' are missing!" and I said, "What do you mean, 'The Stars and Stripes' are missing?"

He explained that they had disappeared from the orchestra folders. The music had been taken away during the night.

At that point people came in from the embassy to wish me well. I told them that "The Stars and Stripes" had been liberated and that we would have to make some kind of decision.

By then I had learned the secret of the kidnapping. In Venezuela there were two highly competitive opera companies. If one scheduled an opera, then company number two would present the same opera the next day.

One company had hired a relatively well known Italian conductor to come and conduct *The Barber of Seville* the week before I was there. He stayed at the same hotel where I was staying. The night of the performance he got a telephone call saying his limousine was waiting for him. Apparently quite pleased that he would have a limousine, he got in the car, a car sponsored, or supplied, by the rival company.

They drove him up into the mountains where they released him. They didn't harm him but he was so far from civilization he could not get back in time for the performance, so it had to be canceled. What the escapade *did* do to this man was scare him so badly that he would not stay to take advantage of the "notoriety and the splendor" he would have received had he performed. He took the next plane out of Caracas.

So I said to my friends at the embassy, "I will do what you say in regard to the Sousa scores. You are going to be here tomorrow; I am leaving. I don't know what the political situation is. I don't want to do anything to make it more difficult. I can refuse to play until the 'Stars and Stripes' are returned—and my pianist did say she would refuse to play until the music is returned—or I can go out and tell the public about this international scandal." After all, it was being televised, and it was the Fourth of July, the two-hundredth anniversary of the birth of our country. I continued, "Or, I can do nothing. I just don't know what would be best. You must make the decision."

They went off to make this grave decision out of my hearing, leaving me thinking it was terribly funny. Every event, from my arrival in the dead of night, the hairdressing salon, the kidnapping of the conductor, to the disappearance of the music—even the parrots—made this whole adventure a kind of never-never experience I am not likely to forget.

They discussed the problem for forty-five minutes. I thought surely they would cancel the concert. Eventually they came back and said they had decided to ask me to go ahead and do the concert and not to say anything about the missing music.

It took me a while to persuade the pianist to play. She insisted that she wanted to get up and make a scene about it, but she didn't.

After the concert I was told that I was invited to dine with the president. It turned out that the gentleman with whom I had the ear-splitting telephone conversations, was not the president of Venezuela, as I had assumed, but the president of the orchestra.

At a big party at the embassy celebrating the Fourth of July, there were eagles made of ice and tiny American flags. I took one of those little American flags, I still have it, as a souvenir. It is my personal "Stars and Strippes" from America's birthday party in Caracas.

That night Arthur Fiedler appeared on television, playing "The Stars and Stripes" from the United States. Although we didn't play it in our concert, the Venezuelans got to hear it after all.

Chapter 16

China

Regardless of where I went to do research, to conduct, or to teach—or all three, as I did in China during the period following their "cultural revolution"—sooner or later there would be repercussions in Boston, usually good, but not always.

At the first rehearsal in the Central Opera Theater in Beijing, I said "Good Morning!" and saw that everybody wrote it down. Everything I said, every bit of coaching I did, they all either noted down or recorded on their tape recorders, and everything I suggested was done.

Now this is a disquieting thing for a normal conductor coach who, particularly when working in a foreign language with an interpreter, expects only a certain amount to get through.

What disconcerted me even more, though, was their apparent lack of interest in anything that was Chinese, and their intense desire to become Westernized.

The opera company had been started by the Russians before their political split ten years earlier. They still had Russian-style sets, as well as Russian-style makeup and costumes.

During the revolution, members of the opera company had been sent out into the fields to learn humility from the peasants. When I got there only about 75 percent of them had come back. The others were so far out, they didn't know it was over and that it was safe to return.

At the end of the cultural revolution, there was only one Western opera in production, so I would be conducting *Traviata*, as they called it, in Mandarin. I conducted several performances of *Travi-ata* in China, which included four different Violettas, several different Alfredos, and four different Germonts.

We rehearsed in a compound that had been assigned to the opera company. When we first went to the theater, to my horror I found twelve standing microphones. I said, "We can't use these. Nobody can see anybody." They explained that it had to be done that way, that people were used to it, and besides, without microphones they could not hear anything.

"In my country," I said, "we do it differently. Sometimes, when we have to use microphones, we wrap them in foam rubber and put them on the floor. The foam rubber keeps the vibration of the feet from getting into the microphone. Because in my country foam rubber is often gray, we call them 'mice.'"

This was ten o'clock at night. We sent the interpreter to deal with the ten technicians. They grinned and nodded, indicating that they understood. The next morning, along the footlights were ten electronic mice, all of whom had mustaches and little ears and tails.

On opening night, all the cast came to see me. They were in heavy makeup and because all were made-up identically, I couldn't tell who was who.

With me to celebrate opening night, was a friend, John Ardoin, a music critic from Dallas. We went out and splurged, buying two cases of champagne, which we collected from various hotels. We took them to the stage manager and explained that it wouldn't be appropriate to use the bottles of American Jack Daniel's whiskey, and Coca-Cola they had provided for the party in the first act, because the opera took place in Paris. We explained that champagne would be appropriate for the party, and here was the champagne. On opening night they didn't open the bottles during the party onstage. They pretended to pour, and saved the champagne for a cast party after the opera.

When we decided to perform Puccini's *Turandot* at the Opera House in Boston we hired Ming Cho Lee to do the sets. In preparation, Ming and I went together to China. It was very exciting for him; he had been born in China but hadn't been back for many years. We spent a lot of time in villages that would furnish inspiration for the decor.

We talked with the head designers of the Central Opera Theater in Beijing and asked them to recommend people to help us. They said that before they could decide whom to recommend they would like for us to come to the same room the following day. We went and found an enormous table with three tall piles of costume sketches in three very different styles.

One was in what I call Japanese restaurant honky-tonk, and another reminded me very much of Russian opera. The third style was elegant. It represented beautiful classical costumes. Naturally, we chose those.

We were introduced to the staff designers. There were about twenty of them. Because these were people who not only designed but who also made things, we discussed costumes. We discussed almost every character in detail, including how many costume changes would be needed. They agreed to design the costumes and have them made by a certain time. We explained how little money we had and they agreed to our proposals for paying them. To them I suspect it sounded generous. We were told when the sketches for the costumes would be ready and they invited me to return to China to see them.

I have never seen anything so beautiful! There was a suitcase full of perfectly mounted individual sketches. They had woven to scale samples of the fabric that they would be using. They said that if I liked they would weave fabric to the scale for a person. They gave me the sketches.

They proposed that the designers come to America to bring the costumes when they were ready. We arranged for them also to bring a choreographer. We made ticket reservations, as we had contracted to do, having gotten special rates for the tickets through the airlines. We let them know when they could come.

Twenty-two people came. None of them could speak English. Not only that, they didn't come on the flight we had arranged. They came on another flight. They sent a cable and said they were so sorry, but they had been worried that we wouldn't know how to make proper arrangements for them since we were so far away, so they made their own arrangements. They came first class!

They assumed, of course, that we would pay. Bob Greene, a member of our board who, with his wife Phyllis, had accompanied me during that first trip to China, hastened to renegotiate the price of the tickets with the airline. Bob had been the first American businessman to set up a factory, a shoe factory, in China after such enterprises became possible, and I suspect he had a hand in my being the first foreigner invited to conduct the Beijing Opera after the cultural revolution.

Those first-class tickets represented the difference between $2,000 for each ticket and seven or eight thousand dollars apiece—as well as the difference between the five or six people we expected and the twenty-two who came. Thank goodness, we had the services of Bob Green to save us from financial disaster.

We got local interpreters to help us. Even though most of the sympathy in our Chinatown was Taiwan-based, they got along fine. The Chinese were busy every moment. We found rooms in a hotel not far from the Opera House and arranged for them to have their meals in a Chinese restaurant.

They were wonderful. Every one of those twenty-two people was necessary. They taught every singer how to wear the costumes, in particular, how to put them on. The costumes were made in the traditional way with many layers. Everybody had two sets of underwear so it could be cleaned. The cast had to learn how to wear the wigs, how to do the makeup, how to do the dancing, how to handle fans, and how to move.

Turandot was a smash hit. The reviews were ecstatic.

I was very conscious when I went to China that I was going to a country with a culture that was much older than mine. They had much earlier than two thousand years ago versions of most musical instruments that we know. They had string instruments, high, low, medium; they had brass instruments; they had reed instruments, as well as far more sophisticated percussion instruments than we have even now. As there are pictures carved on the walls of caves depicting groups as large as two hundred performing for the emperor, they must have had music.

Some friends from the Boston Symphony had been there before me. They had gone to a museum where they heard some chimes, three octave chimes, that had just been excavated from tombs. These chimes were tuned to a tempered scale.

That seemed almost an impossibility, as the tempered scales we know are considered the basis for Western harmonic music—and as every American schoolchild knows, are somehow related to Bach and his "Well-Tempered Clavichord." We assumed that a very sophisticated mathematical formula went into the construction of the well-tempered scale. The possibility that the Chinese had a well-tempered scale two thousand years before Bach was extraordinary to contemplate.

I was also very interested in their music notation system, which was totally different from ours. Ours, I think, is very poorly constructed. For example, with pitch, if you are going to construct a system on a ladder basis of notes going off, then at least what you see and what you hear should have an equidistant effect. The more information you have by eye is useful in order to know whether it is a whole step or a half-step that you are going up. It's just a poorly constructed typewriter keyboard, as it were, and that's why it's difficult for Western people to learn.

The Eastern music notation system, I had been told, and I had read, was far better because it contained more explanation than our notation system does. It is an interpretation of the marginal relationship between music and text, and freedom of rhythm and all those things that we hand down supposedly from one musician to another.

I wanted to learn more about it, and in doing so, I encountered some unexpected information. The Chinese notational system was no longer being taught in the schools. They were teaching the Western system instead.

There is a Chinese orchestra that plays on early Chinese instruments. On those instruments they play music by Monteverdi, Glinka, and other composers whose music is popular with the general public in the West. It would seem to me more appropriate for them to play music written for the ancient instruments. Chinese composers these days are for the most part writing music that could have been written by Glinka.

At the Beijing Opera, you hear squeaky high-pitched voices. The practice is only a hundred year old, and it's something of which they seemed rather ashamed. But there are other kinds of opera companies that use what is called natural-voice singing. I asked questions about such companies but got evasive answers.

As I was leaving China, my car was stopped on the way to the airport. A young man handed me seven books through the window. He said "These will help you. Do not ask my name," and he left. They are descriptions of various pieces from classical Chinese musical theater.

Since that time I have tried to initiate a project to go to China for two purposes. One would be to attempt to better understand the Chinese notational system and to try to find works that were written in that system. The other purpose would be to find out as much as possible about musical instruments that were used in the past.

There is a musicologist who recently wrote a book in which he said that he has now found something like thirty different sets of chimes in different excavations in China, so obviously the ones I saw were not just happenstance.

I went to a lady who was a Chinese music specialist at Harvard. She told me that this was all nonsense and that it was just coincidence that they had these chimes and that they never used them for anything. She said it was just nicer if I didn't bother about it.

I spoke with a professor at Columbia University who had a program in Chinese arts. He said he would be happy to go with me on a trip to China. But when I asked him to give me the names of other scholars who might also help me, he said he couldn't do that, but he would go with me. We would simply have to find time when he could go; then it would be done through his foundation, and it would cost only $75,000, which I would have to provide. That was not a possibility for me.

Later I would be assisted by the Library of Congress in doing research in the field of ancient Chinese music.

Chapter 17

The Philippines

I had been in the Philippines, where I had been asked by the State Department to go and conduct master classes in music, for only a few days when I received a telephone call from the American ambassador, who said that Imelda Marcos, the wife of the president, wanted to give a dinner in my honor. I asked, "Should I accept the invitation?" and the ambassador assured me that it should be a wonderful experience. "We'll pick you up," he said, "We'll take you there."

The ambassador spoke with enthusiasm about what wonderful people President and Mrs. Marcos were, how they were misunderstood, and how all they really needed was a good press agent. He said that they did a great deal of philanthropic work but didn't want to tell people about it, that they were proud of giving but didn't want it to appear that it was being done to enhance their reputation. From my talks with the ambassador I got the impression that these were good people. He told me about money they had given for medical research and money they had given to develop a certain strain of rice together with one of our universities. This rice was going to do fantastic things for the Philippines.

In the palace there were photographs of Americans whom I recognized, of Ronald Reagan as governor of California, of George Bush, and of Dwight Eisenhower. It seemed to be a really pro-American establishment.

At dinner, I found myself to be sympathetic to the things Imelda Marcos told me, particularly because I had just come from

China where I had been very much discouraged by the fact that the people I dealt with there had seemed interested only in becoming Westernized.

Mrs. Marcos said that a number of people had given them very beautiful paintings for a museum they would soon be building for which they had found land and had raised money. In the meantime, they had one room in the palace especially treated so the air and the atmosphere would be appropriate for the paintings. Offering to take me to see these gifts, she observed, "It's absolutely ridiculous to have them all here."

"Before I am willing to let this museum be built, before my people have access to seeing all the beautiful things from other countries, I want them to take pride in what is being done in the Philippines, so they will not be intimidated by art from other countries. For that reason we have built eight small museums throughout the country in which works of our people are on display. Paintings and works of craftspeople are carefully displayed in them so our people can take pride in them. I want you to visit them."

I did visit three of them and found that they were beautifully done. They weren't pretentious but they certainly fulfilled the concept of Philippine culture that seemed to me very important.

I heard about the attempt to build a cultural center in the Philippines and how Mrs. Marcos's husband had absolutely refused to help because he felt it wouldn't be appropriate for the government to fund such a project. When enough private money was assembled, he gave them land that had to be filled in before it could be used. She was very amusing in her story about how she thought he had done it just to get the land filled. They did build the cultural center, however.

Her father was a teacher, so Imelda Marcos did not come from a rich family. As wife of the president, wherever she went in the Philippines, she dressed well, never dressing down for the people, she explained, expecting them all to aspire to a good standard of living themselves.

She told me how she tried to create jobs for people of the Philippines, particularly encouraging them to develop things they could do with handicrafts. In this effort designers had been brought from America as well as from France and Italy. "They settled on designing shoes. They were very successful but the terrible thing was that far too many people began making shoes."

And, continuing, "Whenever a new shoe is made by a manufacturer I am given a pair and I have to wear it. I can't throw the shoes away because if I do, somebody will be offended, therefore I have the world's largest collection of shoes! Sometimes I wear two or three pairs of shoes in a day so I can show my loyalty to the various Philippine craftsmen who learned to make shoes in beautiful styles."

Later on, when all the Marcos's problems came, we read about her shoes as if they represented some aberration on her part. There were other examples of unusual behavior reported in the press that I understood in a very different context.

I was taken to a musical colony up on top of a mountain, where they educated young children mostly. There were not enough pianos but there were plans to supply more. When things went awry and nine Steinway pianos were found in the palace, I suspected they were not for the Marcos's personal use, but were destined to be used by students at the conservatory.

I returned to the Philippines again at the request of USIA (United States Information Agency), this time with other Americans, remaining several months helping with the musical part of the cultural program.

Mozart's *The Magic Flute,* an opera for which I have a special affection because I found a copy of the original manuscript in the desolation of East Berlin after the end of World War II, was the opera chosen.

The Philippine stagehands were taught how to build scenery using American techniques. There were various training programs and, because of the content of the opera, people in different clergies, including the Jesuits, the cardinal, the Methodist bishop, and the Anglican bishop were contacted. They were very supportive of what we were doing.

While I was busy with the production of the opera, Jim Morgan, my assistant, led an educational program. During our months there he went into several schools where he was encouraged to do anything educationally he wanted to try. He worked with crippled children, and with orphans, and he went to the diplomatic school, as well as to the poorest schools. Kids whom he taught and with whom he had developed projects came to the performance of *The Magic Flute.* They were well prepared, and understood what they were hearing and seeing. Several American singers came to join the Philippine cast for the performances in Manila.

When my time in the Philippines came to an end, and I flew back to America, I happened to be seated beside a young American who was on his way back to school. His summer job had been to distribute money to people who were using new methods of farming. He said, "You know, Marcos broke up some of the big plantations held by landowners, and assigned plots to people if they would use good techniques to get better rice production."

The American government subsidized this to a certain extent. The young man's job had been to go out and look at crops in Block B and to see if they were being raised in accordance with the new techniques. If so, he was to give them money. He said it was almost hopeless with older people but young people were enthusiastic. They understood that new crops farmed by new methods were better, but it was very difficult for the old-timers to change. He spoke about how much he had learned to respect what they were trying to do.

After we returned to Boston, Mrs. Marcos helped to arrange a program in which we took twenty Philippine musicians and singers and planned an educational experience for them. Nobody was interested remotely in their political affiliations. They all had different programs based on their specialties and their needs. Some musicians needed coaching, some singers needed language instruction, some singers needed to learn how to act, or to learn music quickly. We prescribed their training, and brought teachers in from Curtis and Juilliard and Boston. The Philippine sponsors paid for them to live in Boston for three months during which time we kept them very busy. It was an excellent program. We did it very conscientiously. Sometimes the singers sang in the chorus, but they were so busy with their studies that they had very little time for anything else.

During that time our theater was picketed by anti-Marcos people in Boston at every performance. They had literature sent in to us by people who entered the theater. Soon they had the community aroused by the use of grotesque, supersize puppets.

We had a talented man in our shop who had good connections at Tufts University where his wife's father taught. Through him we heard of an expatriate from the Philippines, a Mr. Aquino, who lived in Boston. He supplied the names of various companies who were willing to be helpful with projects related to our Philippine students. In other words, he was helpful, but never ever was there any political pressure of any kind put on us to use one person or not to use another person.

There was a big meeting at Harvard set up by one of the divinity faculties. There were people there from Amnesty International. I explained that USIA and the State Department had asked me to go to the Philippines for a musical cultural program. People seemed to be contemptuous of anything that had come from our government. I explained that there was nothing political about anything we did or said while we were there.

In the back row sat Mr. Aquino. I said, "Mr. Aquino, please take me out of politics. Please explain that you helped us. While there may be many things everyone needs to lament in the Philippines, I don't know, but this certainly isn't one of them." He got up and walked out.

Mrs. Marcos came to Boston sometimes because she was having trouble with her eyes. She would go to the eye doctor, and I would be invited to go up to his office, and we would talk. Before Benigno Aquino left for the Philippines, she said to me that she had just met with him, and that they were very much concerned that he was planning to return to the Philippines: "My husband would welcome him back although they disagreed politically. We think he would be a good follower, but we have urged him not to come now because there is so much tension. The Communist forces have created a number of problems. We can't guarantee his safety. We have begged him not to come for several months. And then when he does come, we hope he will let us invite him."

A few weeks later, Mr. Aquino returned to Manila. He was shot and killed at the airport.

In the crowd of people who were picketing our theater was a group of at least a hundred clergymen who held a prayer service on the Boston Common. They prayed that Sarah would give up this dreadful enterprise of helping with the musical education of Philippine students. At the same time these things were going on in Boston, we were getting letters from Jesuits in the Philippines, from the Methodist bishop in the Philippines, and from various clergymen whom Jim Morgan had met, all of whom wrote such things as, "Please, don't give up the program! It's the best thing that has happened. It provides a wonderful opportunity. It gave hope and it's a marvelous project. If you give up, even music will become political."

On Good Friday before Easter, together with Ferdinand Marcos, I was burned in effigy on the Boston Common. There were huge figures, newspaper accounts, and pictures.

We met, finally, the people who were behind the demonstrations. There were three people, all Americans, who spent much time and energy doing this. Two of them, I thought, were quite sincere in their hatred. We had their pamphlets.

Laszlo Bonis, who was then president of our opera company, insisted that we be courteous, and we always were. We served coffee to them sometimes.

The two leaders came to me, a man and his wife, and said they would like to see the opera we were presenting, if there was a way it could be arranged. I said to them, "Well, look, I'll tell you what, if you will promise not to distribute any pamphlets, that you won't take any pamphlets into the theater, I'll invite you to come to the opera as my guests. We'll ask you to leave the pamphlets with a person backstage." And they did.

We talked to the State Department and they sent people to investigate. These people decided, without any question, there was political motivation, probably relating to events concerning Mr. Aquino.

We had a meeting with some of our trustees and representatives of Amnesty International at the Harvard Faculty Club. By that time, I had bought enough books to learn quite a lot about the situation. Someone at that meeting said to me during a question period, "How can you reconcile what Amnesty International tells you about the horrors in the Philippines with your program?"

I answered, "Well, I don't think they are related. I don't challenge what they say. I haven't seen the horrors myself, but I don't challenge what they say. On the other hand, I have read a great deal about Amnesty International's program.

"If you say that we cannot educate young Philippine artists here, then I have to tell you that we can't have any music at Harvard, or at Cambridge either, and certainly not in Concord. If you read of the atrocities that are happening at the Concord reformatory [and I had a whole list of Massachusetts complaints], there can be no museum in Lexington, no museum in Concord, and no museum in Cambridge if an accusation by Amnesty International of bad behavior means that you can have no music."

Later on, when we met with Amnesty International, they said that I had given a great report and they wanted to make sure we didn't think they were behind all this.

After Ferdinand Marcos and I were burned in effigy, all the nonsense died away with the embers. We finished the program. We countered the accusations of the campus with our own explanations. But it was unpleasant. It was particularly unpleasant for some people on the board, but I was proud of the way they backed us up.

The brother of Imelda Marcos was Philippine ambassador to the United States at that time. He called me and was very upset. He had heard what was happening in Boston and wanted me to know that he was sorry that we were taking punishment for trying to do nice things for his country.

Later on, after Marcos was deposed, the ambassador came to an opera at Boston with his daughter, who was going to an area school. They came backstage, but he wouldn't stay. We tried to get them to remain for a conversation, but he behaved as if he didn't want to be recognized.

There was a time when President Marcos himself came to the United States and spoke to the United Nations. At that time Noel Velasco, a tenor from the Philippines, who was an artist-in-residence with the Opera Company, and I were in New York. We were invited to a townhouse that President Marcos owned. We joined Mrs. Marcos and twenty people from the Philippines for lunch. Waiting for the president to come back, which he did sooner that anyone expected, we listened to him speak on television.

He said to me, "We are going to have an opera company in Manila," and he turned to everybody in the room and said, "And you're the board and she gets all the help she needs!" It was pleasant, but no one took it terribly seriously.

Soon I read all kinds of terrible things about Ferdinand and Imelda Marcos and their excesses. It was hard for me to reconcile those accounts with my personal experience with them.

Chapter 18

The Soviet Union

Before cultural relations between America and the Soviet Union were broken off as a result of the Soviet invasion of Afghanistan, I had been invited by the Ministry of Culture to visit the Soviet Union for two weeks. In Moscow and in Leningrad I was encouraged to examine three opera companies to determine if I might feel comfortable doing opera with one of them.

I'm sure the process included their looking me over while I was supposed to be looking them over. We agreed on when I could be expected to return. Then, at the end of 1979, Soviet troops entered Afghanistan.

Although official cultural exchanges had been canceled, I received a telephone call from Moscow asking me if I would come and do it anyway. I said I would have to think about it. Then I got a call from someone at the State Department saying that they understood that I had been approached, and that they wished very much that I would not return to the Soviet Union to work with an opera company. As a matter of fact, they asked me not to do it, and I thought, "Well, they know a lot more than I do. I'm a citizen of the United States, and if the State Department says don't do it, I won't do it." I was surprised to have the State Department contact me because I hadn't told them about my telephone call. I hadn't told anybody. I had been keeping it to myself, wondering what to do.

When the Russians contacted me again, I said I was bitterly sorry but I would not be able to come, that it was just not possible at that time. I did not tell them that my government had asked me not to do it. I somehow had too much pride, both for my government and for myself. Anyway, the collaboration didn't happen and I suspect they guessed why it didn't happen.

Several years later, after Mikhail Gorbachev had become head of the Communist Party and the Soviet Union indicated that its troops would be leaving Afghanistan, cultural contacts became possible again.

Rodion Shchedrin, a composer whom I had met in Moscow, was one of the first cultural figures to come to America. In New York he gave a press conference in which he said one of the people he wanted to talk with was Sarah Caldwell because he wanted me to perform his opera, *Dead Souls*, and he hoped I would get in touch with him.

Several people called to tell me about this. I talked with him on the telephone and went down to see him. The result of our discussion was that I was invited to come to Moscow to discuss the possibility of doing something with Rodion. I very much wanted to produce his *Dead Souls* in Boston.

In the Soviet Union there was an organization called the Union of Composers. During difficult, changing, and often monstrous times, the members kept meeting. Because of his strong Communist affiliation, the director of this union for many years was held in scorn in many places of the world.

Although we heard that certain composers were not allowed to write music on certain topics, the reality was that they were not permitted to perform their works in public. It was assumed that a lot of serious music was being written privately, secretly.

Rodion assured me that much interesting music was at that time being composed in the Soviet Union as composers were beginning to feel freer to express what they wished. He confirmed that much music had indeed been written during the time when it could not be performed publicly.

I went to Russia as the guest of the Union of Composers and met a lot of composers. I was wined and dined and entertained every night. When formal events were over, about ten o'clock, we went out visiting composers and performers at their homes.

The concept for an exchange festival began with a conversation with Rodion Shchedrin. I suggested that I bring four or five people from Boston when I came to conduct and that he do the same when *Dead Souls* would be presented in Boston.

He suggested that we add music of other composers. The idea that began as an opera exchange quickly became a small festival that would take place in both countries. In our imagination it grew bigger and bigger as we met several times in his apartment in Moscow.

I got to know his wife, Maya Plisetskaya, the world-famous ballerina, and she, too, agreed to participate in the exchange.

I met Lev Ginsberg, the music critic, writer, and friend of Rodion and was taken to his apartment. At one point Rodion said, "Wouldn't it be good if we could get Lev to come?" He spoke excellent English, so I said, "Lev, you must come!" and he said, "They'll never let me out. Never in my life will I be able to leave the Soviet Union." In the end, he did come. He was master of ceremonies for the festival and stayed for several months. When our project was initiated, many people, like Ginsberg, were convinced that it could not happen.

For the next trip I was able to get some foundation money and took with me a young representative from the Massachusetts House of Representatives, Nick Paleologis. As a result of his trip, he became so enthusiastic about the idea of a festival and all the things that could happen that he came back and introduced a bill in the legislature that got us $500,000. On the basis of that, we realized that the festival would be possible.

The first thing we did was hire the most meticulous person I knew, John Cunningham, as our money manager. In my artistic life, I have never been willing to take on the responsibility of signing a check unless it was my own check with which I was paying for something.

The protocol drafted by Paleologis included a provision for the sending country to pay travel expenses, salaries, and compensation, while the receiving country would handle local transportation, housing, food, venues, provide additional performers, and sell tickets. That way no money would change hands between the participating groups.

It took many trips and many meetings with different unions in the Soviet Union. When we finally reached an agreement, every element in that agreement was kept.

One thing not included in the agreement, however, but that had been promised, turned out not to be possible. It became a great blow to the return festival when the Soviets were not able to arrange for charter planes to come and collect the Americans and bring them home again.

Just before the protocol was signed for the music festival (by then, I had been to Moscow many times, negotiating arrangements with different ministries and unions), I thought we were through. We had been told in secret and in confidence that if Ambassador Matlock would make one call to one person, everything would be all right. He solemnly went away and made a call and came back. There was to be a final meeting the next day.

As I was on my way to what I assumed would be that final meeting with the minister of culture, I was told there was another group with whom I would have to speak.

I was escorted to the meeting, which took place in an enormous room in an enormous building. There I was confronted by a room full of people whom I had never seen before. They looked as if normally they sat there covered with dust. Occasionally the dust blew off when the door opened and somebody came in. They had certain things in common. They were gray. Their skins were gray. Their suits were gray. Their looks were gray. I felt like I had wandered on to the set of a bad play.

It was not the Ministry of Culture. It was some other ministry. These were much older, sterner people than I had talked with before. They seemed to know nothing about the exchange although I thought the agreement was ready to be signed, sealed, and delivered. I was expected to explain everything once again.

Try as I might, I couldn't get anyone to smile. They were like actors in a silent movie.

Finally one old gentleman stood up. It obviously took a lot of effort. He looked at the others and then asked me, in great seriousness, "What will happen if one of our dancers decides to defect?" Everybody looked very grave.

We had never discussed this. I had a moment of inspiration. I said, "It's really very simple. This is an exchange festival. You have a few people you would like to get rid of, and we probably have a few people we would like to get rid of, and we can trade them." The whole place went up, they laughed so hard. That was the end of that. The agreement was signed.

When the Wang Center in Boston heard that we had gotten a grant they wanted it turned over to them. They wanted to run the festival. There were some powerful Bostonians on their board.

We also had a fine board of our own, many of them retired CEOs. They got so angry at their colleagues that half of them resigned to teach them a lesson. I didn't see that it was teaching them a lesson; I saw it as leaving us in the lurch.

There was a moment when I was sitting in my office in the theater with a man from Washington who ran an independent office set up by President Reagan to handle exchanges with the Soviet Union. I received a call from a man in a law firm in Boston who was trying to raise money for the festival because the initial fund-raising group had not raised enough. The head of Boston Edison had promised to raise the money but he had not been able to raise all we needed.

The lawyer called to tell me that he had just gotten a call from the secretary of state, asking him to tell the big Republicans in Boston that they needed to help pay for this festival or it would be a terrible embarrassment. Hearing this, my visitor, Greg Guroff, looked at me, and I looked at him and he said, "Never in a million years!"

I was called later by the *New York Times* and was asked if it were true that the secretary had made this call. I said, "He didn't call me, but I have heard that he did make such a call. I don't know." This was followed by the lawyer calling me and saying, "Under the circumstances you are not to be allowed to speak to the press about anything." I said, "I have not contradicted or in any way implied that your telephone call did not happen. I only said that I wasn't there." We did not hit it off very well after that.

As our exchange grew, we lost control of the number of people participating. The idea took over the actuality so that in the end we had three hundred Soviet artists in Boston! There were more than a dozen composers, twenty-five dancers from the Bolshoi Ballet, twenty-five members of the Bolshoi Orchestra, and an exchange of students, including twenty students who came and spent six weeks at the New England Conservatory.

The press in Boston ran articles about the ineptitude and lack of fiscal responsibility that I was showing. Although most didn't read English, someone must have told some of the leading people of the exchange about this, because they called a press conference and said a lot of positive things about my having sponsored Making Music Together. I appreciated that.

Although the Boston commissioner for the arts, Bruce Rossley, and I had gone to Washington several times to try to get federal support for Making Music Together in Boston, we were unsuccessful. We would be more successful in getting assistance for Making Music Together in the Soviet Union two years later, but that, too, would be a struggle.

At USIA we were told that they had money only for very small projects. When I wailed, "There must be some place in this government that we can get some help!" someone suggested—facetiously, I suspected—that we should try the State Department.

Then and there I picked up the phone and called the office of Roz Ridgeway, whom I knew. She was assistant secretary for European affairs and had been American ambassador to East Germany.

She came right to the phone and said, "Sarah! Come right over. Come to breakfast!"

She told Secretary Shultz about our project; as a result I met him several times. Once, when he was going to be in Moscow and I was going to be in Moscow, he said "We'll go somewhere and have a secret meeting." I liked him.

Soon I was invited by Mrs. Obie Shultz, a delightful lady, to have lunch with Mrs. Shevardnadze, wife of the Soviet foreign minister. It was a ladies' luncheon, very like those my great-aunt or my grandmother would have given. I remember as a child that ladies would come wearing gloves and hats. They were received in one room where they were offered a glass of sherry. Next, they were invited into the dining room for lunch, which was basically chicken salad and iced tea.

The gathering was held in a historic house just outside of Washington. At first I wasn't sure why I had been invited, but then I realized that it was because I had been going to Russia and because I knew something about music. Mrs. Shevardnadze was known to have musical connections and a daughter who was a musicologist.

I was seated at Mrs. Shultz's table with Mrs. Shevardnadze. I talked with her about her daughter the musicologist, then I asked her if she had had a chance to do any shopping. She said no, but that she wanted to shop. Mrs. Shultz was pleased to hear that, because she had to deal with this lady through several days of activities. We talked about where she might find the items she wished to buy.

Then I said I loved to shop in Moscow. Mrs. Shevardnadze laughed and said, "What on earth can you find in Moscow?" I said that from my last trip I came back with a pelmeni press. She thought that was terribly funny and she gave me her personal recipe for pelmeni, a kind of dumpling with meat inside.

Soon I was invited to go to the Union Republic of Georgia, the home of the minister of foreign affairs and Mrs. Shevardnadze, to conduct an opera. Unfortunately, trouble broke out in Georgia and I was not able to go.

We had two years to take deep breaths and try to raise money before we went to the Soviet Union for the second half of Making Music Together.

We received a line-item grant of a million dollars from the State Department, but the USIA, which administered it, decided to keep $100,000 for other programs.

There were two volunteer groups working in Boston on behalf of the festival in the Soviet Union. One was organized as an operating company and it had a small board. The other was a fundraising group. Dr. Rhys Williams, the person who had lobbied very hard to get the line item, was in charge of fund-raising. He, being a nice, generous, warm man, told a representative of the USIA he would make every effort to raise the additional money so they wouldn't have to give up the hundred thousand dollars. He worked very hard to raise money, as did other distinguished people in his group.

It was difficult to do at that particular moment of economic downturn, but Rhys Williams devised a scheme that we expected to bring in at least $150,000 and potentially twice that. It was to be a trip for Bostonians to travel to Moscow during the festival. People who booked it knew that their doing so would support the festival.

You have to take your folks along if you are to have financial support for international concerts so they can travel with and be proud of their performers.

All kinds of special things were organized. Arrangements were made for them to spend two nights at the dacha of the Bolshoi Opera. The Russians were going to open certain portions of museums that were not normally open. It was to be a very special kind of trip, that couldn't be bought by money. They were to go to the Bolshoi to see the opera we produced there, Robert DiDomenica's *The Balcony,* and to attend a number of concerts.

We were invited for a reception at Spaso House, the residence of the American ambassador. Those people were going to have an extraordinary trip. Everything was meticulously planned.

We had begun to sell tickets when suddenly people were warned not to travel to the Soviet Union. This was at the moment in 1991 when the Gulf War began. The State Department issued an advisory against going there.

With Ted Koppel and the State Department telling us not to go to the Soviet Union, it was hard to think that we should do so. We canceled the trip for Bostonians to visit Moscow to participate in the opening there of Making Music Together. That meant that funds we expected to receive did not materialize.

All our performers came, however. I don't think we were ever under any danger. Our ambassador participated by reading Aaron Copland's *The Lincoln Portrait,* which had been translated into Russian by the poet Andrei Voznesensky. Ambassador Matlock did this although his staff preferred for him not to do it for security reasons.

We did not have the presence of Leonard Bernstein as we expected. I had worked with him on his *Mass,* which we planned to present. It was a real theater piece. It had a big chorus, a rock band, and a jazz group, together with a lot of soloists. A young tenor was to play the guitar and sing and there were thirty-two small parts in addition to a boy choir. We were saddened when he died, and dedicated the first Moscow concert to him.

We also expected Mikhail Baryshnikov to return to Moscow to dance. He had defected several years before. Although he planned to come, we could not make the complicated and expensive arrangements the American Ballet Theatre demanded.

Most concerts during Making Music Together, particularly those in Boston, were the result of collaboration. If it was a chamber music concert, it was rehearsed and prepared by both Russians and Americans. The operas were presented by joint casts. The festival orchestra was made up of Russian students and professionals and American students and professionals. It was an excellent orchestra and we had several different conductors of both nationalities conducting.

I suspect that in Russia they knew more at the time than we did in America about contemporary American music. Much more was played in Leningrad and in Moscow and in Siberia than had been played in Baltimore and Detroit and Los Angeles.

The contemporary operas that were the original focus for Making Music Together remained the centerpieces for the exchanges. *Dead Souls* by Shchedrin was presented at the Opera House in Boston and *The Balcony* by DiDomenica was presented at the Bolshoi Opera in Moscow.

The Balcony, which is based on an antiwar play by Jean Genet, and uses the dialogue of the play word for word, takes place in its entirety in a brothel in the midst of a war zone. The chief of police is one of the main actors. The content shocked the Bolshoi conductor so much that he walked out, denouncing it as immoral.

Shchedrin, his friend, questioned whether we should have performed it in Moscow. Although he had been very active in arranging Making Music Together in the United States, he seemed to lose interest in the return engagements in the Soviet Union. I began to suspect that his major interest had been in having his *Dead Souls* produced in the United States and arranging for his wife, Maya Plisetskaya, to perform his "Carmen Suite" in Boston.

After the performance of *The Balcony*, the minister of culture came to me and hugged me and said it was the most exciting moment they had had, that it showed the Bolshoi their limitations. He was impressed that our singers did not look at the conductor, and that they could act as well as sing.

The festival opened officially in Moscow and continued for many weeks in different locations across Russia. The first concert, however, was held in Saratov. After a twenty-four-hour train ride, our group of more than thirty people were met by the mayor and the conductor and led to the opera house on foot. There we were offered fresh bread and coffee. The orchestra was on the stage waiting for us.

It happened that the Gulf War of 1991 began the day of our performance. I came on the stage and said, through an interpreter, that news of any war is sad news. Then I said that we mustn't let anything come between our countries to make us enemies again. There was applause and a standing ovation.

The most important result of Making Music Together, in my opinion, was the interaction between Americans and Soviets, the artists and the audiences.

During that time we saw remarkable political changes. At the end we were dealing no longer with the Soviet Union, which had self-destructed, but with the Russian Federation.

After Making Music Together was over, we sent very detailed copies, far more information than anyone would want to know, about Making Music Together to USIA. We sent copies of all the programs, many copies of reviews, copies of the letters we wrote, a whole record, and I was called by someone in the USIA and told we had done a good job.

The $100,000 was never made up. We were expected to contribute a certain amount, and with the grant from Congress, the State Department was supposed to supply a specific amount.

That became a major bone of contention. While I was doing the artistic report, a financial report was made. After the financial report was filed, an investigation of our finances was begun. USIA claimed not to have the information we had filed.

Meanwhile, our theater, where all the original papers had been stored, was vandalized, and a lot of the records were missing. There was evidence that the vandals, who had lived for a time in the theater before their presence was discovered, had used papers to make fires on the concrete floors. Fortunately bank records were available.

We continued to suffer because we were unable to make peace with USIA over the facts that we didn't raise as much money as we were supposed to for the grant and that they didn't give us all the money we were supposed to receive.

Rhys Williams wrote beautiful, clear, explicit, heartbroken letters about how the trip by supporters from Boston had been arranged and why it had to be canceled. Had that trip gone off, we'd have had enough money to cover the money that had been taken from our grant.

I am proud of the accomplishments of Making Music Together despite all the problems—even despite the fact that ultimately the stress from Making Music Together meant that the Opera Company of Boston could no longer perform, and that the Opera House had to be closed.

In a world where technology seems to have overtaken humanity, it's imperative that we continue to communicate. That was the basis for launching our festival. The exchange worked on a very simple principle: the most important thing one can do in this world is to enable people to keep talking to one another. Even though the performing artists lived in different countries, held vastly different political ideas, and spoke different languages, that didn't matter. Through music they communicated.

Chapter 19

Yekaterinburg, Russia

I have been invited often to Yekaterinburg, Russia, as chief guest conductor for the Urals Symphony Orchestra, formerly the Sverdlovsk Symphony Orchestra. Its name was changed when the city reverted to its pre-Soviet name of Yekaterinburg.

After Making Music Together was completed, while I was conducting in Leningrad, which was soon to become St. Petersburg once more, I was asked by the deputy minister of culture if I would like to be invited to Sverdlovsk to conduct.

I agreed at once because I was curious to hear that legendary orchestra that performed in a closed city. I said I would be very happy to go to Sverdlovsk to conduct.

The Sverdlovsk Orchestra had not participated in Making Music Together, but I had heard that the orchestra was contemporary composers' favorite orchestra because they did not object to preparing concerts of modern music. Rodion Shchedrin had told me that it was one of the best orchestras in the Soviet Union.

For my first performance in Yekaterinburg—"A Festival of the New World," they called it—I brought Sarah Reese, a wonderful soprano, with me from the United States.

Getting there was an elaborate process. First, we had to get to Moscow. We had a small American grant to enable us to do that. In Moscow, we were put on a train that took thirty-six hours to arrive in Sverdlovsk. We brought enough food for a week and made good use of the samovar that was boiling at all times as the end of our car. The train was comfortable and clean. There was a

Sarah recruits singers fron church choirs in Yekaterinburg for Verdi's Requiem

woman who seemed to do nothing but clean the floors and the bathroom. In Sverdlovsk, Sarah Reese and I shared an apartment. There was a woman there who looked after us very well and cooked for us.

I found musicians in Sverdlovsk who were dedicated to music and who performed superbly despite difficult conditions—including not receiving compensation for weeks at a time. That would cause many orchestras to disband. They received the equivalent of thirty-five dollars a month while we were paid the equivalent of one hundred dollars in rubles for each concert. That meant we were paid what amounted to three months' salary for each musician.

I was invited back often and over several years arranged programs of many kinds. My relationship with Sverdlovsk (later renamed Yekaterinburg) has been interesting. I have had to raise money to get there and I have had to raise money to get other

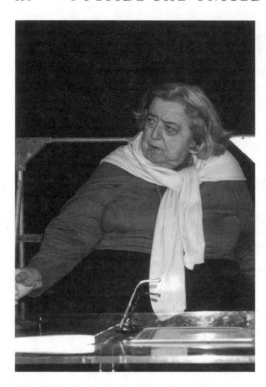

Sarah coaches the chorus for Verdi's Requiem

people there, but I loved it, particularly when I was busy. I was so happy making music there. The people I worked with are wonderful people.

We did the first performance in Russia of *Pelléas and Mélisande* by Debussy. We did Verdi's *Requiem.* We prepared a von Weber concert, and we prepared Bach concerts. We performed concerts of American music, including several concert performances of *Porgy and Bess,* a special favorite there. All the performances of *Porgy and Bess* were sold out long before we got there.

The organizers of Making Music Together had wanted us to bring *Porgy and Bess* as part of the festival, but we felt that it was time the people learned that there was other American music that was just as good. The pleasure that *Porgy and Bess* gave to the audience in Yekaterinburg was quite special, so I'm glad that we did it there.

We took three American performers and presented an evening of Negro spirituals. We announced that concert the day we arrived to take place a few days later. It sold out in a day. For the performance there were hundreds of people who had been unable to buy seats standing in the back of the hall, listening. There was a great emotional reaction to the spirituals. Rhythmic clapping of the audience started early. There were shouts. The singers were touched by this.

One December we presented an evening of Christmas music for an audience that didn't know any of the songs. We played a suite that had been orchestrated by the Philadelphia Orchestra and arranged by Phillip Harris. We treated it as a symphony. The orchestra was enchanted, as was the audience.

I managed to find the score of music written by Prokofiev based on the Pushkin poem *Eugene Onegin*, music that had never been performed. I very much wanted its world premiere to be in Yekaterinburg with the Orchestra of the Urals.

Prokofiev lived in Paris for a while. He was persuaded to return to Moscow by a theater director named Tairov. He was

Sarah conducts Verdi's Requiem *in Yekaterinburg*

Women's chorus selected by Sarah for Yekaterinburg performance

commissioned to write music for a play based on Aleksandr Pushkin's long poem, *Eugene Onegin*, which was to have been performed on a Pushkin anniversary, but had not been.

In the Tairov Theater, which was an experimental, obviously very political, theater, there was a playwright who had written the play. It was organized a little differently and it was a brilliant play.

The score by Prokofiev to accompany the play was published in his complete works. There was a lady musicologist who decided that Prokofiev had no right to write incidental music for a play, and had no right to have anything to do with anything that changed Pushkin, so she took the music and she pasted the poem over it.

I went to the Prokofiev Archives in Moscow and I found the original score of this music. I also found the copy of the play that Prokofiev had used. It made very clear where each musical piece that he wrote was to be performed and for what purpose.

We produced this poem set to music in costume in a beautiful production in Yekaterinburg. The fact that the musicians and members of the ballet and people from the theater who participated were not paid, however, became a scandal that led to litigation.

This is what happened: I was taken to the minister of culture in Yekaterinburg, who promised the money to pay for the performance. Then Mr. Kholotursky, manager of the orchestra, lined up all the people we needed in addition to the orchestra—people from the theater and from the ballet—and hired them. We had a splendid performance of the piece that had never been performed before anywhere. Meanwhile, the minister was fired and there was no money to pay the performers.

Among the soloists invited to go to Yekaterinburg was a young woman named Carolyn Staley, who had been a neighbor and friend of Bill Clinton during their youth. When she told the president she was sorry his mother had died, she mentioned that she was going to Yekaterinburg to perform with the orchestra there. He responded by saying that he would be in Russia at the same time, and wouldn't it be fun if they could get together?

The president asked the people who were planning the summit meeting between him and President Yeltsin if the orchestra could be brought to Moscow to play while he was there. It was arranged for twenty-four members of the orchestra to perform during a reception to which cultural leaders would be invited to meet the president, at Spaso House, the residence of the American ambassador.

We were told that there was concern that Carolyn Staley's singing might focus attention away from the president. Someone, in fact, called Carolyn and asked her not to sing. The president telephoned Carolyn in Yekaterinburg from Vienna and said that

The men's chorus Sarah selected

Sarah tries out the drum

he was looking forward to hearing her sing. She explained that she had been asked not to. About an hour later a call came from Moscow, asking Carolyn please to sing.

It was suggested that I not conduct the orchestra, that I just let somebody else do it from the side so I could come to the party to meet the artistic leaders of Moscow. I, of course, did conduct.

The ambassador and his wife were charming to us. Everything went well. We did not overshadow the president at the reception. President Clinton smiled and shook hands and talked with everybody.

We had been told that there would not be enough food to feed the orchestra. I said that we had no intention of asking that the orchestra be given refreshments. I knew many of the people on the Spaso House staff, so I was not surprised when cold drinks appeared. When the reception was over, trays of marvelous sandwiches and pastries and coffee materialized. A table was set and the Spaso staff entertained us.

As artistic director of Making Music Together, which had taken place a few years before, I knew composers, conductors, performers, poets, painters, and writers, many of whom I had met in that very house. I asked to see a guest list because I wanted to know which of my friends would be coming. I was appalled to see that on the list of the so-called cultural leaders of Moscow that there was only one person I would consider worthy of the title. She was a poetess who did not come.

The thing I found distressing was that there seemed to be no sequence of contacts. Former ambassadors must have left lists of guests whom they had invited. It was quite clear that this ambassador and his wife, who were new, had not had the opportunity to make connections in the artistic and intellectual communities. The people who had been invited were basically midlevel administrators of various organizations, not artists themselves. I found it surprising that there was no continuity. If it is not the system within embassies that personal contacts be continued, I think that system ought to be changed.

For almost everything I wanted to do in Yekaterinburg, I had to take music. It cost me a lot of money because I had to buy the music. Finally, I spoke with a friend at Kalmus (the firm that supplied the music) who wanted to know about certain Russian scores for which they did not have orchestra parts. They thought the scores might be available in Yekaterinburg.

I got the Yekaterinburg Library to make a list of such music and sent it to Kalmus. We worked out a deal whereby they were allowed to copy the music to rent. In return, the orchestra in Yekaterinburg was supplied with the music it needed.

I also tried to help the orchestra solve their problem of less than perfect instruments through gifts and donations from America and France. Some I arranged for them to buy for reasonable prices. We set up Friends of the Urals Symphony Orchestra, through which people could make contributions and donate instruments to the orchestra.

We took a violin maker to Yekaterinburg to repair instruments. His name was Doug Cox, but to Russians, he was "Duuug." He offered to take one of the young musicians in the orchestra who had been helpful to him and train him as a violin repairman. The orchestra was very excited about that. They offered to provide the money to send the young man to America to learn the craft of repairing violins.

The Trust for Mutual Understanding let us have $7,500 to bring the musician who wanted to learn to be a violin repairman to America.

Doug Cox arranged for the young man, whose name was Volodya, and who could hardly speak English, to come to America to study the craft. His coming was predicated on his learning English. He never believed it would happen. He just couldn't believe that he would be able to travel to America, but at the last minute he crammed and went to the American Consulate and applied for a visa to study in America. They didn't believe he spoke English, so a visa was denied.

When I called the consulate and asked why they were doing this, I was told that they were afraid he would stay. I said, "Come on, he has two young daughters and a wife!" Then they asked, "If he doesn't speak English, how will he get along?" And I said, "He speaks enough English!"

I called the person who was head of the program at the University of New Hampshire and explained the difficulty to him. He said, "Sure, let him come. We can manage."

Finally, he was allowed to go for ten weeks. He studied both in Boston and at the University of New Hampshire, which had a violin repair summer studio. Then he apprenticed in the shop of a master repairman.

He turned out to be the star of the summer. Doug called and said that he was doing exceedingly well. He said, "We're going to bring him to live at my house with my family and he is going to work in my workshop and I'm going to give him special attention and teach him things I haven't taught anybody else."

He did nothing but work. He worked all day long and he worked very, very hard. He had a per diem for daily expenses (food, toothpaste, and things like that), which he carefully saved to buy instruments and tools.

Because the orchestra paid for his transportation, there was money left of the grant. I suggested that we buy tools with the extra money, one set for him and one for the orchestra.

He returned to Yekaterinburg to find that the concert hall was being renovated. In addition to painting and bricking over the wall where there were windows through which one could hear trucks rumbling past, a nice workshop was being prepared where Volodya could work at the craft at which he had become skilled.

Lacking an assistant who can write in Russian, I have a technique for dealing with this problem. I dictate precisely and carefully into my "dragon dictate" machine in English and it writes in English what I say. I press a button and my English is immediately translated into Russian. In order to determine whether the translation is accurate, I press another button, and whoosh, the Russian is translated back into English for editing. Then it's translated back into Russian for transmission by fax to Yekaterinburg. It does not do things idiomatically, but the meaning comes through. It's a lot better than inaccurate, or nonexistent translators!

I would like for the Urals Symphony Orchestra to develop a reputation as an international orchestra. This would be unusual for a Russian orchestra. The Russians have wonderful orchestras, but when they tour they often perform familiar Russian music, such as Tchaikovsky piano concertos and the Fourth Symphony, rather than programs that give a real feel of the depth and breadth of the incredible musical legacy from that country.

There was warmth and a sense of appreciation, not only from the players and the administration of the orchestra, but from the townspeople of Yekaterinburg also. It is very unusual, very special, and I have never felt that kind of warmth anyplace else. The performers I have taken with me all came home with this same feeling, a sense of pride and dignity and appreciation that money doesn't buy.

BACK IN BOSTON

The acquisition of the Opera House by the Opera Company of Boston proved to be not unlike the experience of a family that inherits a stately house while not independently wealthy. It would appear a grandiose symbol that would make a lot of people envious; actually, it would become a money pit that could bring about insolvency of the recipient. Renting it out for special purposes would not pay all the bills.

When my husband and I returned to live in the United States, Sarah asked me to become a member of the board of directors of the Opera Company of Boston. I agreed, with the understanding that I would be of use in any way I could—so long as I wasn't expected to contribute financially.

I am an experienced photographer, therefore I made photographs at her request on various occasions. I photographed students from the neighborhood who cleaned and repaired parts of the interior of the Opera House. One of those young men was so pleased to be photographed he reached in his pocket to give me a present. It was a New York City subway token.

I agreed to help record and edit her memoir. Over a period of several years we worked on the manuscript. We worked on it in Lincoln, in New York City where my husband and I lived, in Washington where we also had a house, on our farm in Tennessee, in Princeton after we moved there, as well as in Yekaterinburg, in Prague, and in Tbilisi, and finally in Freeport, Maine.

In New York, Sarah could get tickets for the Metropolitan Opera as if by magic. We went to hear *Tosca* with Luciano Pavarotti. I thought it was marvelous, but she grumbled about singers continuing to sing when they were out of physical shape and when their voices were no longer at their peak. Obviously, she expected perfection in everything concerning opera. I began to

Sarah's productions in Boston inspired in Professor Glen Bowersock a lifelong love of opera

understand her preference for not seeing operas that were staged and produced by others.

Again, I was overwhelmed by hearing Plácido Domingo as Otello. Sarah was disappointed in the opening scene because she thought it defied logic. We went backstage and had a conversation with Domingo while he was still in costume. Because of the other people who were backstage, I was not surprised when it was soon announced that he would become director of the Washington National Opera at the Kennedy Center.

When Sarah visited in Princeton after we moved there, I invited one of the admirers of her productions when he was a student in Boston, Professor Glen Bowersock, from the Institute for Advanced Study, to come and have dinner with her. Although they had never met, they had much to discuss; seeing her performances in Boston had kindled his lifelong appreciation and support of opera. He read her manuscript and made suggestions about its presentation.

We had lunch with my friend, Helen White, who, when she was Helen Shaner, had, like Sarah, been a music student at Tanglewood during World War II. Together with us was Arlene Jones, who also had been at Tanglewood, and had worked with Sarah when she taught at Boston University. In conversation they re-created the ambience of that time. Helen was very helpful in reading an early draft of Sarah's manuscript and correcting my phonetic spelling of the names of certain of their teachers. When Sarah dictated, I preferred not to interrupt by asking how to spell names I didn't recognize.

At the Princeton Museum, Sarah was intrigued with an extensive exhibition concerning Chinese calligraphy, history, and art.

I made several international trips with Sarah. After the disappearance of the Soviet Union, she became chief guest conductor in Yekaterinburg, Russia. I accompanied her and four American soloists when she conducted Verdi's *Requiem* there. The orchestra was superb, but a large choir was needed and there wasn't one. Sarah didn't let that deter her. We simply went to church services, where she listened for the best voices and in her inimitable way recruited individual people to sing for her. Within a week she put

Sarah shares stories about Tanglewood with Helen White and Arlene Jones

The house on Beacon Hill where a concert version of Porgy and Bess *was presented*

together a magnificent *Requiem* that a visitor said to me was superior to the one he had heard the night before in Moscow.

I climbed onto the catwalk beside the stage to make photographs of individual performers performing. She insisted that I also use a small, hand-held movie camera to photograph the entire stage as well. I was inexperienced at that. When she saw afterward that I had photographed the chandelier, thinking it was Sarah, she didn't ask me to do that again.

When the USIA of the State Department invited the governor of Sverdlovsk Province, together with Mr. Kholotursky, Sarah's primary contact in Yekaterinburg, to visit America, Sarah agreed to host them in Boston. I went up on the train a few days early to work with her on the memoir, and Jack flew up the day that she planned a vocal performance of parts of *Porgy and Bess* in their honor. Dr. and Mrs. Jerry Austin offered their spacious home in the historic part of Boston for the gathering of more than a hundred people. The stirring performances of Reginald Pindell as Porgy, and Myra Merritt as Bess, proved to be Sarah's last presentation in Boston.

Just once I observed Sarah's legendary last-minute disorder, which tended to drive many people to distraction. Between breakfast and noon, when she expected to leave for Boston, while she dictated information for this book, she handled numerous other things simultaneously. She took personal responsibility for things most people would have passed on to someone else, expecting arrangements to be made at least the day before. One was the matter of props for the afternoon performance. After a few telephone calls they were assembled.

Myra Merritt and Reginald Pindell as Porgy and Bess

She also worked on the logistics of how to get everybody to the performance on time. She wanted to be there early; my husband needed to be met at the airport; the members of her staff who had assembled at her house in Lincoln would have to get to Beacon Hill, as would the out-of-town performers, and the guests from Russia. Only two cars were available.

While she was dealing personally with these logistical problems, the young lady who was to sing the part of Bess telephoned from her hotel to say that she had a stiff neck and might not be able to sing. Although there was no backup singer, that did not faze Sarah. She assured the young woman that she would ask her personal doctor to call her to discuss her trouble. She murmured to me that it happened all the time, that it was a form of stage fright and that the young lady would be fine. She called Dr. Joe Gardella, her neighbor and friend, who in turn telephoned the performer, discussed her difficulty with her, and offered to give her a prescription for something to help her throat relax if she found it necessary. After all the attention, she found that she did not need to take anything.

Sarah decided to send a member of her staff with me to pick up Jack since, as she said, I knew what he looked like. She drove in early with another member of her staff who was asked to drop her off and then collect the performers. She decided that it would be inappropriate for the Russians to be transported in the jeep of the brother of one of her staff members (which had been volunteered without his knowledge), particularly as the brother was someone who had never driven in Boston. She telephoned for a car service to pick them up, and relegated everybody else to the jeep, assuming they could help him find the correct address, as well as a place to park.

Without losing the thread of the dictation that she had begun before these interruptions, she continued to dictate until it was time to leave.

As the guests arrived for the concert they were greeted by an incongruous surprise. In the spacious entrance hall sat a woman playing a glass harmonica, an instrument many of us had not seen or heard before. If there was any correlation between a glass harmonica and *Porgy and Bess*, I failed to understand what it was. It proved, though, to be a delightful icebreaker for the audience as they assembled, and the Russians were entranced. It was a typical unexpected juxtaposition provided by Sarah.

Everybody arrived on time, the performance was very good indeed, and everything went smoothly.

The next day Jim Morgan and I went along with Sarah to accompany the governor and the manager of the Sverdlovsk Symphony—by then, called the Symphony of the Urals—for an interview by the *Boston Globe*. We were as impressed as they were by the new building. Sarah told them how very much the Opera Company appreciated the finesse with which the *Globe* consistently covered their productions as well as their difficulties.

Our efforts to make sure that the governor returned to Yekaterinburg with a good impression of America and of Boston did not have a lasting effect. He was dismissed from his position shortly after returning home.

Soon after that visit, I traveled with Sarah to Prague in the Czech Republic where she had been invited to lecture to a Czech and American audience during an American Embassy–sponsored evening. In her lecture, she recounted her long experience with performing Czech opera, beginning with Bedřich Smetana's *The Bartered Bride*, her first production. She explained how helpful the Czechs had been in assisting her research concerning other operas, including Béla Bartók's *The Miraculous Mandarin* and *The Wooden Prince* (two of the first operas the Opera Group performed), and Leoš Janáček's *Makropulos Affair*, based on the Karel Čapek story about eternal youth. She went into detail about her unusual production of Robert Kurka's *The Good Soldier*

The opera house in Prague, where Sarah did research for the first opera she conducted

Schweik. She explained how fortunate she was to have worked with the great Czech set and costume designers Jozef Svoboda and Jan Skalický and several incredible opera singers.

We called on Czechs with whom she had collaborated in the past, including Eva Hermanova, who was head of the Czech National Opera. She had helped Sarah with research many years before, when they were both students.

Sarah pursued the idea that *The Bartered Bride* was written as a political statement and that Marinka represented Czechoslovakia itself. She got help from an English-speaking Czech student whom we met in a coffeehouse (that seemed to serve mainly Czech beer).

We ate at the Good Soldier Schweik restaurant where Sarah, the comedian, posed outside, taking on the persona of Schweik himself. We went to see *Eugene Onegin*, but left at the first intermission because the production did not meet her standards. Besides, I was afraid her light snoring would distract members of the audience.

The American ambassador and his wife had us for dinner at their palatial residence, together with Czech conductors and other musical people, some of whom I had known earlier.

Sarah had arranged for us to stay in a private home, a home that overlooked the beautiful Vltava River (better known by its German name, the Moldau), something that would not have been permitted ten years earlier when my husband was American ambassador in Prague.

She went to sleep and slept for two days, barely rousing herself to eat. I became increasingly concerned because I knew that at least once she had been hospitalized with sleep apnea. Suddenly springing back to life, she was ready for new adventures.

Our last trip out of the United States was to the Republic of Georgia. I had been invited to attend an international arts festival, where I had a photographic exhibition. Sarah wanted to extend an invitation to the Georgians to participate in a Library of

Sarah has tea in Prague with an old friend

Sarah takes on the persona of Schweik in Prague

Congress plan for preserving ancient musical manuscripts. Nanuli Shevardnadze, the wife of President Eduard Shevardnadze, entertained us at dinner and introduced Sarah to her daughter, Manyana, a musicologist. They agreed to work together.

We had lunch with Maestro Giya Kancheli who had participated in Making Music Together. The artistic director for the Tbilisi Opera arranged for Sarah to audition three opera singers and invited us for lunch in his spacious apartment, which was filled with stage furniture from various operas. She agreed to return to conduct in Tbilisi.

By the end of our trips, Sarah always managed to have more bags and bundles than she and I together could carry. We had a remedy for that. She would limp, and when we asked for a wheelchair, one was invariably forthcoming. She had one phobia that led to searches in many places for freight elevators: she hated escalators.

When Sarah came to Washington to receive the National Medal of Arts from President Clinton, we stayed at our house in Georgetown. There were other recipients as well, which meant that there were speeches, some of them rather drawn out. I kept willing Sarah not to nod off as she often did when things got a little slow, particularly if it was warm. I had seen her do that not long before in Boston, at a luncheon for a woman conductor from China with whom she had worked in Beijing.

After the ceremony I saw a friend who had also attended, the widow of Senator Fulbright of Arkansas. I introduced Sarah. Harriet, who headed the Fulbright Foundation, invited us to stop by her office, which we did.

Within a few days, Sarah received an invitation to come to Fayetteville to head the opera department of the University of

Sarah lunches in Tbilisi with Georgian composer and conductor Kancheli

Arkansas as a distinguished professor. She accepted the opportunity, sold her house, and returned to live in Arkansas.

Having virtually completed her memoir, she made no effort to have it published. She preferred to wait until reopening of the Opera House was scheduled, thinking it would be appropriate for her book to appear at that time.

The Opera House finally reopened after a multimillion dollar refurbishment, not with grand opera as Sarah Caldwell had envisioned, but with *The Lion King*. She was not invited to attend.

Chapter 20

Difficulties and Options

We believed initially that it would be the greatest godsend for the Opera Company of Boston to own a beautiful theater, but ultimately it wasn't. It was a very old building with many problems. There were problems with the electricity. And with the plumbing. And with the ventilation. Funds after funds after funds had to be poured into the theater—with few visible results.

Nevertheless, for the first two or three years after we moved in the Opera House we managed to pay the actual cost of maintaining the building by rentals to folk singers, to dancers, to whomever needed it for an evening. That was great until we were confronted by more and more problems requiring more and more money.

I was annoyed when I overheard someone in the audience complain about how I was letting the theater go to wrack and ruin because I didn't take care of the cosmetic detail of repairing the seats. In reality we had poured ten times the amount such repair would have required into the theater for the roof, for the heating, for whatever was most pressing at the time.

As we were beginning to think that we had no choice but to close it down, a very interesting thing happened. We were presented with a proposal that made us think that all our financial problems would disappear. The solution was to have come with a plan in which the city of Boston, with the assistance and the approval of Mayor Flynn, and Bruce Rossley, commissioner for the arts, would buy the Opera House from the Opera Company for enough money to get us completely out of debt and provide us with funds to continue producing opera!

The State of Massachusetts, in 1988, promised to hold a bond issue to raise enough money to enable the city to buy the Opera House and also to provide enough money to renovate the theater. It was a much negotiated and much discussed topic. We all signed off on it and were going to sit around a great table and give the deed of the Opera House to the city in exchange for an agreement that gave us free use of the theater six months a year for fifty years. With such an endowment and with a restored theater, we assumed that we would prosper.

We decided that never having had enough money for a full-time manager, we should employ someone who really knew about national companies. Although some people didn't like him, at my insistence we hired a man who had been head of one of the divisions of the National Endowment for the Arts. He came to my house and sat in my living room and assured me that he would work just as hard with the opera company as I had. With the assistance of his lawyer, he negotiated an incredible salary and an incredible contract.

He brought with him a friend, whom he put in charge of subscriptions. As soon as he arrived, our new manager tried to get rid of the people who had been working with us, some as volunteers, and brought three highly paid people to be his assistants. The idea was to create an administration that would be strong enough to handle the transition to the gorgeous, incredibly restored theater we were expecting to have. We planned for a larger company and a longer season.

But there was no bond issue.

We went to the city and to the state and said, "We need money. On the basis of your promises we have made carefully thought-out plans, and hired people to work with us."

"Well," they said, "We're just postponing it until the election. But to show you our good faith we'll set up a loan for you through the Thrift Fund." This was a banking organization owned or controlled somehow by the state.

The city put up some parking lots, and a loan of $600,000 was negotiated for us to tide us over for a few months until the money from the bond issue was available.

Mr. Dukakis did not become president, the Massachusetts economic bubble exploded, and suddenly Boston felt that it had become the most impoverished area in the whole world. All we got from the city for our promises and expectations was a $600,000 debt.

Our administrator decided that he would get rid of me. It was time, he thought, for me to retire. Some of the people with whom he worked were concerned enough about his activities that they went to the chairman of the board and said that they thought there should be an investigation into his capacity to lead. Three trustees were given this responsibility and the conclusion was that he should be let go. I was given the choice of firing him or letting him resign. I said, "Let him resign."

The day after he resigned, taking with him a few people from our board, he started an opera company. The problem was that he didn't know enough about producing opera to succeed. He didn't know how to handle unions; he didn't know how to handle people. But he had sympathy from people who considered him a man whom I had squashed. They got together some money. They rented the Colonial Theater, a beautiful theater that seated about 1,200 to 1,400 people. It was totally union controlled, with union hours, with union stagehands, with union teamsters, and with union ladies in the ladies' rooms.

After only one production, *The Marriage of Figaro*, which they hired Peter Sellers to stage, they disbanded. I was not surprised, because the productions of my friend Peter Sellers are the personification of something that I find disturbing these days: staging opera in a different way just to be different.

Our own financial problems became insurmountable. When there was no money to produce a new opera and no money for

The Opera House is shuttered

heat, the trustees had no choice but to close the Opera House. I borrowed heavily on my own house and sold my front yard to buy the mortgage from the bank so the Opera Company would not be forced into bankruptcy. We did not go bankrupt, and we continued to try to raise money to pay off debts.

The Opera House stood empty and shuttered for several years. Even so, along with old friends and new friends of the Opera Company of Boston, I never gave up my vision of a refurbished and vibrant new beginning for serious opera in the Opera House on Washington Street.

The chief asset the building had was the dedication of people who continued to give their time and their money to help preserve it. When foreclosure was a possibility because of our inability to pay off loans from the bank, when I had already raised as much cash as I could, all of the members of the board of trustees (with one exception, the daughter of our original benefactor) paid off the notes they had signed, and one of the other trustees and I paid off her note for $25,000. Her brother had earlier told me that he would pay all our debts if the Opera Company would not perform any more, but we were not for sale.

The press, particularly the *Boston Globe*, consistently gave excellent press coverage to attempts to revive the Opera House, publishing well-placed, well-researched articles when it was appropriate.

Outstanding opera singers who had worked with us expressed their hope that the Opera Company of Boston and the Opera House would continue to function and that they could perform with the company in Boston again.

The Opera House was placed on a list of the eleven most endangered places in America. The History Channel on television carried a segment about this during one of its inaugural broadcasts.

The Opera House continued to have problems, in part, because of its location in a decaying part of Boston where patrons at times were concerned about their safety in the streets.

A few months after the building was closed, we discovered that a group of street people who called themselves Camelot had made their way in and occupied the building. They sabotaged records

Graffiti takes over the marble façade

and computers, they vandalized costumes, they built fires on the concrete floors, and took out parts of crystal chandeliers and brass railings, presumably to sell.

One summer we had a grant to employ young people, many of whom might otherwise have spent the summer on the streets, to clean the building on the inside. They did an excellent job under the supervision of Ben, the dedicated caretaker of the building. To celebrate their accomplishment, there was a party in the Opera House, to which their families were invited. They were proud to have photographs of their doing this work on display.

Because there was no money to heat the building, pipes burst in the winter, pouring down destruction in several areas. Guard dogs were left to roam the building at night to make sure that that new squatters did not enter the building. By day, Ben was always there. Until he became ill.

When Ben died in the fall of 1997, members of the board saw to it that he had a dignified burial service on his native Staten

These young men are proud of cleaning the opera house

They salute Ben, the caretaker who led their effort

Island (just as they had ensured that he had good medical attention during his terminal illness).

After years of negotiating with various groups that wanted to renovate the building, the city of Boston decided which to choose. I agreed to sell my mortgage. I signed the papers.

They agreed to let us use the theater for several weeks each year. We were promised that a hundred thousand dollars would be available each year for several years to help pay for producing opera. We would have the privilege of naming the Opera House. I thought it would be appropriate to name it for the family that had made it possible for us to buy it. We would also have naming possibilities for various parts of the theater and for the backs of chairs.

We kept waiting and waiting and waiting. But nothing happened.

I began to think that we wasted much time that we should have spent doing opera. All the years we tried to find a way to refurbish the theater, we should have been raising money to produce opera. We should never have stopped performing. We should have performed in church basements if necessary, but we should have kept our company going.

In retrospect, if I had it to do over again, I would go immediately back to the magic wandering years and I would keep presenting opera. But I didn't. I decided we had to save the Opera House and that we had to get out of debt. I was bound and determined, maybe wrongly, that we were not going to go into bankruptcy because I wanted to maintain the dignity of the Opera Company of Boston.

Afterword

When options presented themselves, Sarah enthusiastically took advantage of them. She worked with the Library of Congress in setting up a program for copying and preserving ancient musical manuscripts in several countries. She helped find and preserve ancient Chinese musical material, and have it performed. She also continued to serve as the chief guest conductor in Yekaterinburg, Russia.

When she was presented the National Medal of Arts by President Clinton, he mentioned that they had both come a long way from Arkansas.

She made archival material concerning costume and set designs available to the Robert Tobin Museum in San Antonio, Texas.

She sold her house in Lincoln, Massachusetts, and moved back to Arkansas to become a distinguished professor of music.

At the University of Arkansas at Fayetteville, she headed the opera workshop. While there she facilitated productions of Puccini's *La bohème*, and *The Turn of the Screw* by Benjamin Britten, and was inducted into the Entertainers Hall of Fame.

She conducted contemporary music by German composer Boris Blacher, at Swarthmore College in Pennsylvania. Boris Blacher was the friend from Tanglewood days who had introduced her to the excitement and creativity of opera in post–World War II Germany.

Having retired in 2003, she returned to New England to share a house in the town of Freeport, Maine, with her friend and colleague, James Morgan.

Sarah consults books in Chinese at the Princeton Museum

When my husband and I visited her there, we approached what appeared to be a modest suburban house. Inside, though, Sarah had worked her magic. Surrounded by the belongings she loved, it was as if she had never left her home in Lincoln.

In Boston she was honored by the New England Opera Club, where she was greeted by friends, some of whom had come from far away, at a beautiful dinner for more than a hundred people. People with whom she had worked, and members of the board of the Opera House, reminisced, and several of her favorite performers sang. I was happy to be able to attend because more people wanted to be there than there was space to accommodate. There were testimonial speeches. There was instrumental music. Three of the vocalists who sang had accompanied her to Russia to perform in Yekaterinburg.

In retirement, Sarah has time to read

Sarah and Rebecca Matlock record Challenges. *(Author's collection)*

Sarah was happy to see many friends in Boston at a dinner in her honor

I made what proved to be my final photograph of Sarah, dressed in great style, and happy to be among her friends again.

At midday on May 27, 2006, sunlight streamed through the magnificently restored stained-glass windows of historic Trinity Church in Boston. The church was filled with people who came to celebrate the life and spectacular accomplishments of Sarah Caldwell, who had died of heart failure on March 23, in Portland, Maine.

The Reverend Hugh Haffenreffer, a personal friend who had been the small boy who participated in the coronation scene of *Boris Godunov,* gave the eulogy. The ceremony was accompanied by music by some of Sarah Caldwell's favorite composers. They were Vaughan Williams, Gounod, Verdi, Bach, Mozart, Copland, and Puccini.

The orchestra included members of the Opera Company of Boston and others from the Boston musical community. The chorus consisted of members of the Opera Company of Boston, the Trinity Church Choir, Chorus Pro Musica, and the Back Bay Chorale. There were two flutists, an organist, and four soloists. The soloists were Barbara Quintiliani, soprano, Gigi Mitchell-Velasco, mezzo-soprano, Noel Velasco, tenor, and Richard Crist, bass.

We left the sanctuary to the rousing sound of "When the Saints Go Marching In," clutching booklets we would treasure. Assembled by her friend, James Morgan, they contained comments by many of her friends and photographs of Sarah from the time she was a small child.

Productions of the Opera Group and the Opera Company of Boston

1958–59
Voyage to the Moon—Offenbach
    First American performance
La Bohème—Puccini
The Barber of Seville—Rossini
The Beggar's Opera—Gay

1959–60
Tosca—Puccini
Voyage to the Moon—Offenbach
Hansel and Gretel—Humperdinck
Carmen—Bizet

1960–61
La Traviata—Verdi
Otello—Verdi
Hansel and Gretel—Humperdinck
Falstaff—Verdi
La Bohème—Puccini
Die Fledermaus—J. Strauss

1961–62
Command Performance—Middleton
    First performance
Manon—Massenet
Die Meistersinger von Nurnberg—Wagner
Rigoletto—Verdi

1962–63
Madama Butterfly—Puccini
The Barber of Seville—Rossini
Faust—Gounod

1964
Lulu—Berg
The Magic Flute—Mozart
I Puritani—Bellini
Madama Butterfly—Puccini
L'Elisir d'Amore—Donizetti

1965
The Abduction from the Seraglio—Mozart
Semiramide—Rossini
Intolleranza—Nono
    First American performance
Tales of Hoffmann—Offenbach
Boris Godunov—Mussorgsky
    First American performance of original version

1966
Don Giovanni—Mozart
Boris Godunov—Mussorgsky
Hippolyte et Aricie—Rameau
    First American performance
Moses and Aron—Schoenberg
    First American performance

1967
Don Giovanni—Mozart
Otello—Verdi
The Rake's Progress—Stravinsky
Bluebeard's Castle and *The Miraculous Mandarin*—Bartok
Tosca—Puccini

1968
Tosca—Puccini
Lulu—Berg
Carmen—Bizet
La Traviata—Verdi
Falstaff—Verdi

1969
Bluebeard's Castle, The Miraculous Mandarin, and *The Wooden Prince*—
  Bartok
Lucia di Lammermoor—Donizetti
Macbeth—Verdi
The Marriage of Figaro—Mozart

1970
The Flying Dutchman—Wagner
The Daughter of the Regiment—Donizetti
The Good Soldier Schweik—Kurka
The Fisherman and His Wife—Schuller
  First performance
Rigoletto—Verdi

1971
Louise—Charpentier
La Finta Giardiniera—Mozart
Norma—Bellini

1972
The Trojans—Berlioz
  First American performance of complete version
Tosca—Puccini
La Traviata—Verdi

1973
The Bartered Bride—Smetana
The Daughter of the Regiment—Donizetti

1973 *(continued)*
The Rise and Fall of the City of Mahagonny—Weill
Don Carlos—Verdi
   Original version in French

1974
Don Quichotte—Massenet
Madama Butterfly—Puccini
War and Peace—Prokofiev
   First American performance
The Barber of Seville—Rossini

1975
Falstaff—Verdi
Cosi Fan Tutte—Mozart
Benvenuto Cellini—Berlioz
   First American performance
I Capuletti ei Montecchi—Bellini

1976
Fidelio—Beethoven
Montezuma—Sessions
   First American performance
The Girl of the Golden West—Puccini
Macbeth—Verdi

1977
Russlan and Ludmilla—Glinka
La Bohème—Puccini
Rigoletto—Verdi
Orfeo ed Euridice—Gluck
Orpheus in the Underworld—Offenbach

1978
Stiffelio—Verdi
   First Amerian performance

The Damnation of Faust—Berlioz
Don Pasquale—Donizetti
Tosca—Puccini

1979
Falstaff—Verdi
La Vide Breve and *Master Peter's Puppet Show*—Falla
The Barber of Seville—Rossini
The Ice Break—Tippett
    First American performance
Hansel and Gretel—Humperdinck

1980
Die Fledermaus—J. Strauss
The Flying Dutchman—Wagner
War and Peace—Prokofiev
Aida—Verdi
Hansel and Gretel—Humperdinck

1981
Faust—Gounod
Der Rosenkavalier—R. Strauss
Rigoletto—Verdi
Otello—Verdi
Hansel and Gretel—Humperdinck

1982
Die Soldaten—Zimmermann
    First American performance
Aida—Verdi
La Bohème—Puccini
Orpheus in the Underworld—Offenbach

1983
Carmen—Bizet
The Invisible City of Kitezh—Rimsky-Korsakov

1983 *(continued)*
Norma—Bellini
Turandot—Puccini
Der Freischutz—Weber

1984
Anniversary Gala
Madama Butterfly—Puccini
Don Giovanni—Mozart
Tales of Hoffmann—Offenbach

1985
Hansel and Gretel—Humperdinck

1986
Turandot—Puccini
Taverner—Davies
  First American performance
The Makropulos Case—Janacek
Tosca—Puccini

1987
Il Trovatore—Verdi
Julius Caesar—Handel
Madama Butterfly—Puccini
Don Pasquale—Donizetti

1988
Medea—Cherubini
Dead Souls—Shchedrin
  First American performance
The Threepenny Opera—Weill
La Traviata—Verdi

1989
Mass—Bernstein
Aida—Verdi
Der Rosenkavalier—R. Strauss
La Boheme—Puccini

1990
Madama Butterfly—Puccini
The Magic Flute—Mozart
The Balcony—DiDomenica
   First performance

Index

Page numbers for photographs are in **bold** typeface.

About the Authors

Sarah Caldwell was head of the Opera Company of Boston when it acquired the building on Washington Street that became the Boston Opera House. She was a pioneer woman conductor who, in 1975, conducted the historic program featuring music by female composers at the New York Philharmonic. In 1976 she became the first woman to conduct the Metropolitan Opera. She performed worldwide and helped to organize the festival Making Music Together, which in 1988 brought musicians, dancers, and composers from the Soviet Union to Boston and arranged for return performances by Americans in several cities in the Soviet Union. She died in March 2006.

Rebecca Matlock is a photographer, an author, and the wife of the former United States ambassador to the Soviet Union, Jack Matlock. She served on the board of directors of the Opera Company of Boston and worked with Sarah Caldwell on her memoir for several years.